There Will Be No Palestinian State

Ziyad Clot

There Will Be No Palestinian State

A Diary of a Negotiator in Palestine

ISBN : 978-2-31501-273-2
© Max Milo Éditions
Collection Essais-Documents, Paris, 2024
www.maxmilo.com

Author's Note

This book was born of a very personal desire to bear witness.

One day I decided to go to Palestine, just to see. My mother's family is from there.

Among many other things, I discovered my grandparents' house in Haifa—my home.

I also encountered the 'peace process.' And I became a witness and a player in the fate reserved for Palestinian refugees in these discussions. And I saw up close the impossibility of realizing a Palestinian state.

Later, in the winter of 2008–09, I found myself powerless in the face of the Israeli army's murderous expedition into the Gaza Strip. Like many, I was appalled by this episode. But like few, I had access to the other side of the story.

I felt it was my duty to share my experience on Israeli-Palestinian soil, and this book is my recollection of that story.

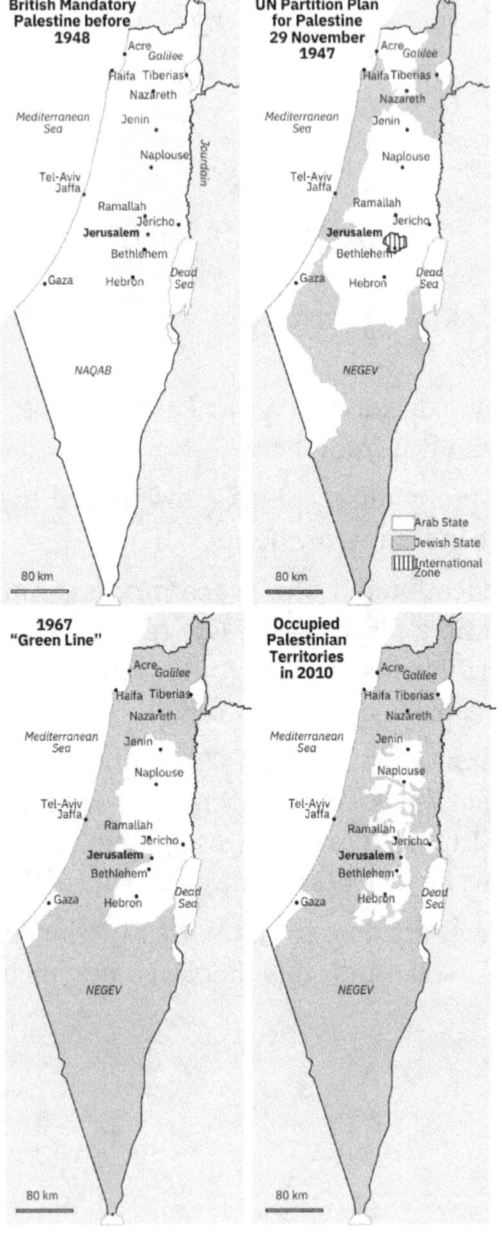
British Mandatory
Palestine before
1948
Acre
Galilee
Haifa Tiberias
Nazareth
Mediterranean
Sea
Jenin
Naplouse
Tel-Aviv
Jaffa
Ramallah
Jericho
Jerusalem
Bethlehem
Gaza
Hebron
Dead
Sea
Jourdain
NAQAB
80 km
UN Partition Plan
for Palestine
29 November
1947
Acre
Galilee
Haifa Tiberias
Nazareth
Mediterranean
Sea
Jenin
Naplouse
Tel-Aviv
Jaffa
Ramallah
Jericho
Jerusalem
Bethlehem
Gaza
Hebron
Dead
Sea
NEGEV
Arab State
Jewish State
International
Zone
80 km
1967
"Green Line"
Acre
Galilee
Haifa Tiberias
Nazareth
Mediterranean
Sea
Jenin
Naplouse
Tel-Aviv
Jaffa
Ramallah
Jericho
Jerusalem
Bethlehem
Gaza
Hebron
Dead
Sea
NEGEV
80 km
Occupied
Palestinian
Territories
in 2010
Acre
Galilee
Haifa Tiberias
Nazareth
Mediterranean
Sea
Jenin
Naplouse
Tel-Aviv
Jaffa
Ramallah
Jericho
Jerusalem
Bethlehem
Gaza
Hebron
Dead
Sea
NEGEV
80 km

I
CHARLES DE GAULLE AIRPORT
SEPTEMBER 2007

I bought an El Al Israel airline ticket.[1]

Destination: Ben Gurion airport, Tel Aviv, Israel.

Sixty years ago, my mother was born a few dozen kilometres away, in Haifa, Palestine.

I bought the cheapest flight I could find on the Internet. Price, however, was of little importance. I forced myself to buy it. For me, this purchase is tantamount to recognition of the State of Israel. Perhaps I should be upfront about it—despite my Arabic-sounding name, I have no reason to hide.

I convinced myself that it was the symbolic dimension of the purchase that prevailed. For me, Israel is a reality, a state I can't ignore. I was raised and educated in France. Its history is my own, including its darkest pages: the Second World War, the collaboration and the complicity of the Vichy government in the Jewish genocide. I didn't experience these tragedies, but they're part of my memory, even if I've reconstructed them from stories.

---

1. El Al is Israel's leading airline.

My father is from Normandy, born in Saint-Pierre-Église, in the Cotentin region. Normandy is familiar—its verdant, rainy charm and family lunches. Due to circumstance, I didn't know Palestine. I recently turned 30; it was time for me to get to know it.

It was time to leave. Or to *return*, I'm not sure. As a preamble to a longer stay, I planned to visit Israel and the occupied Palestinian territories. I wanted to find a job there. I'm a lawyer, and teaching law at a Palestinian university, for a year or more, seemed like a sound project within my grasp.

My Israeli friends warned me, 'You must be at the airport for check-in at least three hours before departure; El Al security doesn't mess around.' With these recommendations in mind, my father agreed to accompany me to Roissy at dawn.

We arrived at the airline's check-in desk at barely five o'clock in the morning at Charles de Gaulle. We were the first ones there in the empty airport . The counters opened about ten minutes later, just a few small desks where young employees conduct their interrogations. In the middle of the old Roissy airport, before dawn, I'm struck by the setting: security cordons have been placed; I can see cameras on the ceiling. It's all a little intimidating.

There, a polite young man greets me. He explains in English that, for security reasons, he's going to ask me a few questions. He asks for my passport; he opens it, reads my name, and looks me in the eye.

'Ziyaaad?' he questions.

'Ziyad Clot,' I reply. 'Yes, that's my name.'
'Why are you going to Israel?'
'I am going there on vacation.'

The questions follow in quick succession: Do I know anyone in Israel? Yes. Where will I be staying? With friends in Tel Aviv. He asks me for their names and telephone numbers. I give him what I have. And in Jerusalem? I'll be staying at a hotel. Which hotel? I tell him the address of the inn where I've booked a room. I show him what it is in my guidebook. He quickly examines the book entitled *Israel and the Palestinian Territories*. He points to the words 'Palestinian territories.'

'Are you planning to go there?'
'No. But I'm also planning to go to Bethlehem.'
'That's in the territories.'

He reexamines my passport. Now he wants to know what I do for a living. I respond that I am a lawyer. In what field? I explain in vague terms that my professional practice is in a Parisian business law firm. Naturally, I don't mention that I've resigned. He asks who my clients are. I reply that I'm not allowed to elaborate for reasons of confidentiality. I only mention that the firm's clientele is made up of international clients, as well as French and multinational financial institutions. That should reassure him.

He'd like me to give him a business card. I hand him the card, as well as that of the Paris Bar. He thanks me, apologizes, and leaves. I see him disappear behind a door that seems to lead to an office, belonging to El Al or to the company that manages its security.

Charles de Gaulle Airport

The young man comes back to me a few minutes later. He picks up the guide and says, 'As a business lawyer in Paris, you make a pretty good living, don't you think?'

The incongruity of the question threw me for a moment. What's he getting at? I awkwardly explain that I have nothing to complain about.

'I don't understand,' he adds. 'If you make a good living, why wouldn't you prefer one of Jerusalem's higher-end hotels rather than a hostel in the Old City?'

I reply, firmly this time, 'I don't think I have to justify my choice of hotels. I don't see what gives you the right to ask such questions.'

He says nothing. I feel compelled to continue:

'Very well. If you must know, the *American Colony*, one of Jerusalem's luxury hotels, was overpriced. I'm going to visit Jerusalem alone; I don't see much point in taking a $400-a-night room.'

'Of course, I understand.'

He leaves again, going back to the same room. I glance away at my father. Immersed in his newspaper, he doesn't see me. The check-in area is now bustling with activity. Many of my fellow passengers have already checked in.

The security guard returns:

'Ziyad.'

'Yes.'

'Do you have another passport?'

'No.'

'Where were you born?'

'It's written on the passport in Paris.'

'But where does your first name come from? It isn't French?'

'My parents gave it to me, what more can I say?'

'What is your father's first name?'

'Jean-René.'

'Your grandfather's?'

'René.'

'Where were they born?'

'They were both born in Normandy, France.'

'Your mother?'

'Jihan. She is of Lebanese descent.'

And there it is... My interlocutor eyes me. I hasten to add that my mother has lived in France for almost 40 years now.

'Have you ever been to Lebanon?'

'Yes, but that was a long time ago.'

'When?'

'Just after the war.

'The war with Lebanon was last year...'

'Sorry, I meant the civil war. It must have been 1991 or 1992.'

'Do you have family there?'

'No, I no longer have any family in Lebanon.'

'Do you speak Arabic?'

'No, just a few words.'

'Do you have any Lebanese friends?'

'A few friends, yes, but most of them live in France.'

'Who are they?'

'College friends, work colleagues.'

'I see.'

Charles de Gaulle Airport

The young man walks away again. I glance again at my father. This time, our eyes meet. I walk over to him and explain the situation. We're separated only by a security cordon that demarcates the registration area from the free world. He looks worried. He points out that the interrogation has already been going on for almost an hour and a half. I shrug and smile, trying to reassure him.

I go back to the desk where my interlocutor meets me a little later. He explains that he needs to call my two friends in Tel Aviv. I pretend not to understand. It's barely 6:30am there, after all. He explains that he has no choice but to follow security protocols. I ask him to wait a little before complying. He points out that the later it gets, the further behind we are in checking in. I have no choice but to acquiesce, but not without asking him to apologize to my friends.

He leaves again. The security guard is careful not to call in front of me. This little game is becoming increasingly suspicious. He comes back five minutes later to say my friends can't be reached.

'People are asleep at this hour,' I said.

He'll try again, he says, always from this hidden room, which now gives rise to my wildest fantasies. Behind this door, carefully locked at all times, I imagine the Mossad,[2] the Shin Beth[3] the CIA, even NASA, all discussing my fate.

In the absence of a telephone conversation with my friends in Israel, the security guard asks for permission to

2. Mossad is Israel's spy agency. It carries out secret operations around the world, including the liquidation of Palestinian leaders.
3. The Shin Beth is Israel's internal security agency.

search my luggage. I tell him I have no objection, of course. He slips away again.

Do I really have nothing to hide? Suddenly I'm trembling. My belongings are now being dissected: will they confirm the statements I've made so far? I try to make a quick inventory in my head of what's in my suitcases. I realize that my luggage contains an Arabic dictionary and some articles I had published in an English-language Egyptian magazine a few years ago. Some of them deal with the Arab–Israeli conflict.

I'm trapped. But alone, and apparently unguarded, since my interlocutor has returned to his hiding place where he and his colleagues are, I'm convinced, now peeling back every facet of my life. I approach my luggage. I look left and right, trying to assess the situation quickly. It's like *Midnight Express*: my forehead beaded with sweat, a few kilos of hashish taped to my abdomen, about to face moustachioed Turkish customs officer. My heart is pounding. I can feel it reverberating in my limbs. Even the artificial light of the boarding hall makes me anxious now. Yet at this moment, no one seems to care about me. With feigned detachment, I open the luggage that could potentially harm me. I take out a book which I pretend to leaf through carelessly. In a flash, I empty the bag of the few suspicious documents and slip them under my jacket.

I text my father on his mobile. He reads the message, raises his head in my direction, and comes over to meet me. I discreetly hand him the magazines and dictionary. He gives me a haggard look. Nervous, I urge him to take the documents and return to his seat. After a moment's hesitation, he complies.

I wait for my executioner. I look at the clock. It's 7:30am. He returns at last. He has news for me:

'Unfortunately, there's a long queue at baggage claim. You're going to be too late to check in.'

He pauses. I'm hanging on his every word.

'You can fly, but your luggage will follow on another flight, once it's been checked.'

I give him a severe look.

'Don't worry,' he continues, 'They'll arrive without fail on tomorrow's flight.'

He pauses again for a moment, then resumes:

'No, sorry, you'll receive them on the flight the day after tomorrow, your luggage won't be able to leave before then. Shabbat starts tonight, so you won't be able to pick up your luggage in Tel Aviv for another two days.'

We're now staring at each other. I decide to put an end to this farce.

'There is no way I can leave my luggage in your possession for two days, start my stay in Israel without my belongings and be forced to go back to the airport to collect them,' I tell him.' If possible, I'd like to get my luggage back now and be rescheduled on the next flight. I hope I'll only have to go through baggage screening the next time I'm here, since I've already answered all the questions you've asked.'

The man leaves to consult what appears to be a supervisor. After a short discussion, they both come back to me. The officer apologizes for the complications, and that he'll get in touch with El Al to see if my ticket can be changed. I nod.

He finally returns and gives me a new ticket; I'm rescheduled on another flight two days later, at the same time.

'Make sure you show up three hours before check-in,' he feels obliged to add.

I swallow my irritation. I just ask him to make sure I don't have to undergo another interrogation. He assures me that my name will be passed on to the next flight's security officer, so I don't waste any time. The two men bid me farewell. Absurd as it may seem, I thank them mechanically.

I join my father and explain the situation. He looks at me, dumbfounded. We return home.

*

Two days later, we set off again at an even earlier hour. We drive in sleepy silence.

I give my name on arrival at the counter. A smiling young woman tries to initiate a new conversation. I interrupt her and calmly explain the situation. She defers to her superior, different from the one I met two days earlier. To my relief, I'll be able to go straight through baggage claim.

As it happens, the checks will be carried out in the infamous locked room to which I've been denied access until now. At last, I'm going to be able to get to the bottom of the mystery, to gauge the Israeli security apparatus from the inside. I'm invited to take my luggage cart through the door. It's a shock. The room is tiny, almost dilapidated. All I see in front of me is an old X-ray machine. Three seats have been arranged on one side. In opposite corner of the room, an

Charles de Gaulle Airport

old curtain hanging from the ceiling seems to demarcate a body search area.

I take a seat. The security officer joins me and explains, in a friendly tone, that the first person will perform the body search, then personally go through my luggage. A handsome young man in his twenties enters the room, tall, athletic and short-haired. He greets me, and in broken English, he invites me to step into in the small booth for a body search.

The man sidles into the narrow stall with me. He performs his search meticulously, leaving nothing to chance. His palpation is active and thorough. Only my genitals escape the officer's expert hands, but he goes right down to the seams of my pants. Strangely enough, the experience isn't as traumatic as I'd imagined.

The young woman now moves on to my two pieces of luggage. She asks me to show her all the electronic equipment I own. Everything goes: the cell phone, the digital camera and the BlackBerry, which particularly grabs her attention. Once again, it's never-ending. Seeing the clock ticking, I ask if someone can take over my check-in in parallel with the search. She assures me that it will be taken care of. Combing through the rest of my luggage takes another half-hour. Finally, she tells me she's finished. I'm in charge of packing my bags again.

I'm handed my boarding pass. With the long-awaited approval in hand, I leave the room and head for my father. My father, who's lost sight of me for some time, finds it hard to hide his deep concern. I reassure him that I'll be able to catch my flight.

This interminable wait gave him time to go through the previous day's *Le Monde* several times. The crumpled pages of the paper betrays the multiple read-throughs to which the newspaper has been subjected. While we're still facing each other, just separated by the same security cordon, my father hands me the daily newspaper, which he suggests I read on the plane. At that very moment, before the paper has even soiled my hands, the Israeli security officer appears behind me—the handsome one, the one I thought had stayed in the search room. He throws his body violently between my father and me.

'No! He's clean. He can't touch anything!'

My father and I look at each other, astonished.

I then understand that the boy doesn't intend to let me go so easily. In fact, I've been assigned an escort. An *escort boy,* rather, given the young man's youthful physique. He now follows me like a shadow.

Since all physical contact with my father is now forbidden, I simply give him with an awkward wave. That's as good as goodbye. Everything else will be a joint affair with the guard. A couple of tall, dark-haired men with a vague family resemblance, not so badly matched, but arousing the astonished glances of the people we pass.

Crossing the airport concourse is a breeze, passport control too. I feel like I'm a minor under guardianship. All I need is a plastic bag around my neck containing my plane ticket and my identity. I wanted to do some *duty-free* shopping. I wanted to go to the toilet. I decide not to. It's not worth the hassle. My freedom of movement is now under close surveillance.

Charles de Gaulle Airport

I finally board the plane. My escort accompanied me to my seat, then nods and leaves. The other passengers stare at me suspiciously. I pretend not to notice and take my assigned seat. A good-natured, ordinary-looking passenger, Sephardic Jew by the looks of it, sits down beside me. He gives me a placid, benevolent smile. I do the same and collapse a few minutes later into the arms of Morpheus. But not before fastening my seatbelt.

Safety first.

II
FIRST MOVES
SEPTEMBER 2007

The captain's announcement snaps me out of my reverie: 'Welcome to Ben Gurion Airport, welcome to Israel.' I grimace, imperceptibly.

The airport is modern. Posters celebrating the history of the Hebrew state adorn the long corridor leading to passport control. A bust of David Ben-Gurion, the father of the Israeli nation, greets arrivals in the Holy Land. It's soon my turn; after barely two minutes, the immigration officer makes a phone call. I'm ushered into a waiting room. In the company of a handful of others, mostly Arabs, I wait, staring absent-mindedly at a TV screen on the wall.

I'm called about twenty minutes later. I pass a new officer. Same questions. Same answers. He asks me for the name and contact details of my acquaintances in Israel, whom he's going to contact. He adds that he would like my telephone number and e-mail address, 'for security reasons.' I acknowledge that I have no real choice and give him my French mobile number and an old e-mail address that I no longer use. I'm sent back to the waiting room, where I wait, again, longer this time.

A woman finally comes to meet me, calling me, once again, by my first name:

'Ziyaaad...'

She hands me my passport, stamped with a three-month tourist visa. I'm good to go—I'm allowed to visit Israel. Well, almost: another baggage check awaits me. This is the last step, this time, without trouble. I've got both feet in the Holy Land.

I easily find the train to Tel Aviv. Loaded up like a mule, I struggle into a carriage. Suddenly, I'm face to face with a group of Israeli army grunts. I look around me: the other civilians in this car can be counted on one hand. Surprised, I find an empty seat amid this gaggle of kids in khaki uniforms that they are struggling to fill with their lanky bodies. The *Uzi*, the Israeli army's machine pistol, hangs carelessly from the shoulder of each of these soldiers, barely out of puberty. They play with their cell phones. They talk in friendly banter. They're just kids.

The train stops at the Tel Aviv–HaHaganah station. It all makes sense: this is apparently one of the Israeli army's camps. The carriage empties in an instant.

I arrive in Tel Aviv under a radiant sun. I meet up with an Israeli friend who gives me a warm welcome. Tel Aviv makes a great impression on me: the Mediterranean, with the air of California. It's not beautiful, but it seems like a good place to live. I take the opportunity to take the plunge. At the end of summer, the beach is deserted and the swimming divine.

Unfortunately, I don't have time to linger. Problems with El Al and the postponement of my departure forced me to revise my itinerary, so I decide to leave liberal Tel Aviv for religious Jerusalem. I jumped into a cab, heading for the thrice-holy city.

*

I wonder about my cab driver. His face, his brown complexion, his thick eyebrows, his dark eyes, his accent, everything seems to indicate that he is an Israeli Arab, a Palestinian. Or a Sephardic Jew. I'm not quite sure. Maybe my eye isn't sharp enough yet. I'm tempted to start a discussion to find out more. But my as yet-unidentified cab driver is hanging on to his cell phone with his mother. And quickly, the landscape flies by. Sleep catches up with me.

When I wake up, we've almost reached our destination. The driver asks me where my hotel is. I tell him it's at the Jaffa Gate. *Yaffo*, he says, in Hebrew. Suddenly, my questions are answered. My driver tells me he's from Tel Aviv; he doesn't know Jerusalem well. He tenses up:

'Is that the Arab quarter over there?' he asks me in English.

'I don't think so, the Jaffa Gate is just one of the gates of the old city.'

'I'm not going into the Arab town. I don't know my way around there. It's dangerous.'

To ease his anxiety, I tell him that all he has to do is drop me off at the gates of the wall.

The city walls are now in view. The cab driver finally drops me off at the hostel, just a stone's throw away. A young

American with red hair and a toothy grin greets me. He welcomes me to Jerusalem, *The Holy City*, as he calls it. I find my room. Its Spartan comfort and uncluttered decor seem conducive to prayer or, failing that, meditation. At the rate things are going, they may soon catch up with me.

Despite nightfall, I decide to go out for a short walk. My map shows the entrance to the Arab souk a few steps from the hotel. I enter an empty, poorly lit alleyway that looks like a deserted market. I quickly turn left into a passageway. The place is just as quiet. I take another alley, this time to the right. My wanderings are suddenly interrupted by a shout in a language I don't understand. I turn around and see two Israeli soldiers wearing bullet-proof vests and each carrying a sub-machine gun. One of them approaches me and asks, this time in Arabic, if I'm an Arab. Surprised by the question, I tell him I'm a tourist, an identity more in tune with my current state of mind.

He stares me up and down and orders me to turn around:

'It's Ramadan. You can't go there. It's not safe. For Muslims only!'

These words, pronounced in heavily accented English, leave me speechless. I turn on my heel and head back to the hotel. I'll have plenty of time to see the old town tomorrow.

*

Waking at dawn, I decide to flee my hostel as quickly as possible. A group of American evangelists have invaded the premises. Let's be clear: I have the utmost respect for religion and believers. My lack of faith, a sad fact after ten years of Catholic upbringing, often leads me to have a somewhat irrational admiration for the pious. This morning, however, the hubbub of the hotel refectory assaults my senses. Dealing with thirty or so pilgrims who are as quick to converse about Christ as I am slow to unstick my eyelids, still glued shut from sleep, is beyond my capabilities.

So here I am, setting off on my adventure in Jerusalem, wandering through its narrow streets, filled with enthusiasm: in the extension of the Armenian Quarter, the Jewish Quarter catches my eye with its cleanliness and the many renovation projects underway. After passing through a security gate, I reach the Wailing Wall below the Muslim Haram El Sharif. Everything intersects here: histories and religions intermingled, battles fought, in the heart of a ridiculously narrow space. Absent faith, I'm afraid I don't feel the extraordinary evocation of the place. But I do have a first glimpse of the difficult cohabitation between communities.

I linger in front of the Wailing Wall. The crowds make the place not very conducive to meditation. Yet it is luminous. It's fascinating to see these believers praying before the Wall. The scene unfolding before my eyes is timeless: it has been repeated for years, decades, centuries. By contrast, the Holy Sepulchre, which I reach a little later, disappoints me. Overflowing with tourists, the vast majority of them South Korean that day, it loses all its appeal because of the circus that takes place. I'm distressed by the lack of spirituality emanating from the site. A stone's throw away, a monastery run by old Ethiopian patriarchs is, in its simplicity and austerity, far more evocative. The Way of the Cross, its little chapels and churches, are also more touching. Were it not for the omnipresence of the army, the journey in the footsteps of Christ would almost be meaningful.

I lunch in the Christian quarter on an outdoor terrace overlooking the old town. The majestic, gilded Dome of the Rock catches my eye. It is the city's most visible landmark. The only thing missing from my Jerusalem tourist baptism is a visit to the Esplanade of the Mosques. I set off again. After a few wanderings through the winding alleys, I find one of the gates to the Muslim holy site. An Israeli security checkpoint faces me.

I'm stopped by one of the two soldiers at the checkpoint. He speaks to me in Hebrew, then in English. He wants to know where I'm going. I explain that I want to visit the Esplanade of the Mosques. He asks for my passport. I hand it to him, and he naturally stops at my first name.

'Ziyad: Arab? Muslim?'

I tell him that my name is Ziyad Clot, that I'm French, born in Paris, and that it's all there on my passport.

He makes a gesture of annoyance and grumbles, more aggressively:

'Are you a Muslim? What's your religion?'

I explain that I'm not going to the mosque to pray, but just to visit the site, as a tourist, after visiting the Wailing Wall and the Holy Sepulchre.

He doesn't let go. 'But, Ziyad, is it Muslim? Is your father a Muslim?'

Then I realize that perhaps the entrance is only open to believers. I stammer out a vague lie:

'My father is Christian, but my mother is Muslim.'
'Fatiha,' he said, 'You know Fatiha?'

I grimace in incomprehension. Who the hell is Fatiha?

'Fatiha?' he repeats again.

I then understand that the soldier is asking me to recite the Fatiha, the opening sura of the Koran. I have vague recollections of the prayer I once learned in Arabic class. I begin to recite:

'Bismillah hir rahman nir raheem / *Alhamdu lillahi Rabbil 'alamin ...*'

I pause abruptly, overcome by a sudden sense of humiliation. The Israeli soldier has forced me to lie about my religion and recite a prayer, in order to gain access to a Muslim holy site to which he controls access. I take my passport back from the soldier. He looks at me, bewildered.

'I've changed my mind. I don't want to go anymore.'

Once again, I'm forced to turn back. It's late now; I need to get back to the hotel. I share my experience with the American receptionist, who is surprised by my insistence on going to the Mosque Esplanade. He tells me that there are probably opening hours for prayer only. We'll have to find out. In my guidebook I spot another entrance that is open to the public before prayer. Tomorrow I'll get up early to make sure I get there.

*

The next day, well before prayer time, I arrived at the entrance to the Mosque esplanade near the Lions' Gate.

This time, I find three Israeli soldiers. Unfortunately, two of them are the same ones I met the day before. They greet me with a wry smile—they recognized me. Another passport check:

'So Ziyad, are you a Muslim or what?'

Irritated, I reply that, outside prayer times, this door is supposed to be open to tourists. A totally fruitless discussion ensued. I stand in front of the gate while a few Palestinians enter the Esplanade. They are elderly people. They're not checked. I brood, exasperated. The third soldier, who had been watching us out of the corner of his eye for a while, now joins in. He's much more aggressive. His Arabic is perfect. In fact, he looks Arab. He explains that I don't belong here if I'm not Muslim. He adds that, if I want to see the Esplanade, I must go through the entrance next to the Wailing Wall, like everyone else.

I leave the scene, irritated, and decide to return to the Wall to use this crossing point, which I hadn't noticed on my visit the day before. There, another soldier points out a suspended walkway, a few dozen meters from the entrance to the Wailing Wall. The gangway is heavily secured. I pass a large number of Israeli soldiers, but no tourists, as I walk through a gate and finally enter the Temple Mount on my third attempt. The Haram El Sharif is on my right, the Dome of the Rock on my left. Between the two, a wide, open courtyard is planted with a few trees. I stop here for a moment, before heading for the entrance to the Haram.

Just as I'm about to take off my shoes, I'm shouted at in Arabic. The man who seems to be the mosque guard asks me where I'm from. I tell him I'm French. He welcomes me, then asks me if I'm Muslim. I had no problem lying to the military, but I'm reluctant to sin at the entrance to a holy place. I try to sway him by telling him that my parents are Christians, but that we Christians, Muslims, and Jews share the same Holy Book. The guard stares at me. He refuses. I insist. He braces himself, nervous, and orders me to move on.

At my wits' end, I slump down a little further away, dejected. Too tall, dressed in Western style, I feel like I've been prematurely judged. I glance around me. On the other side of the Esplanade, children heckle as they leave the *madrasas*.[4] Closer by, two Palestinians, employees of the *waqf*[5] no doubt, are gardening. One of them greets me with a nod. I take the opportunity to ask him why the entrance to the Haram is closed to non-Muslims. He says he's sorry, but the entrance has been closed to tourists since Ariel Sharon visited the site in 2001. The provocation precipitated the second Palestinian Intifada, and since then, the *waqf* has been adamant that no non-Muslims may visit without special authorization.

*

Despite my frustration, I decide to go to Ramallah. I take a cab at Damascus Gate, on the East Jerusalem side. The jovial Palestinian driver is full of greetings. For the first time since Tel Aviv, I smile again.

---

4. Koranic schools.
5. The *waqf is* the organization that manages religious property.

First Moves

Ramallah is only a dozen kilometres from Jerusalem; it's practically a continuation of the Holy City. As we approach what appears to be an Israeli roadblock, my driver makes a sudden U-turn to take a side road that descends steeply. Suddenly, we're off the beaten track. The road, whose asphalt had previously been perfectly maintained, gives way to an old tarmac path where the cabbie dodges potholes, despite the narrowness of the carriageway and the oncoming cars. I ask where we're going. My cab driver explains that this is the only road leading to Qalandiya,[6] the *checkpoint* that separates Ramallah from the Jerusalem conurbation.

The road passes through a surprisingly quiet Arab town, but there are no signs to indicate that we're heading for Ramallah. We turn right, then left, and come face to face with the 'wall.' A few graffiti adorn the massive concrete edifice. We turn left. My cab driver tells me that the wall divides Palestinians in two—it separates families, prevents the movement of workers and cuts Jerusalem off from Ramallah and the rest of the West Bank. The suburbs close to Ramallah, located in the continuity of Jerusalem and those to the west of the wall have been driven to desolation. On my right, the wall, whose course the road continues to follow, winds for some two to three kilometres. The town to my left is deserted, as if dead. Only the flow of cars bears witness to nearby human activity.

Images of the Berlin Wall, which fell on 9 November 1989, naturally come to mind. Half-serious, I ask my driver

---

6. See map of East Jerusalem and surrounding area, p. 94.

if he thinks it's possible to demolish the Israeli 'security fence' with a pickaxe. He laughs and tells me I can always try. He hastens to add, however, that we're right next to an Israeli military zone. I later learn that the wall is made up of several layers of concrete and metal. Thermal cameras have also been installed to signal any suspicious movement.

We arrive at the Qalandia *checkpoint.* This modern building looks more like a tollbooth, or even a border post, than a security checkpoint. Crossing to the other side of the wall is a shock. Even if the geographical continuity between the two sides is undeniable, the first glimpse of this territory left to the Palestinians gives me the impression of a dump placed in the middle of chaos. Concrete blocks and barbed wire litter the ground, and garbage piles up everywhere. There's no apparent logic to the direction of traffic. I look up and see an Israeli watchtower perched on the wall to my left.

The cab was no longer able to avoid the craters riddling the road. His car's shocks strained. Compared to the beautiful Israeli roads, it's night and day. Traffic is at a complete standstill due to the state of the pavement. Deadlocked, honking in all directions. My driver explains that the road hasn't been resurfaced since 1967, when the Israeli occupation began. The authorities of the occupying force have always opposed the idea. This first section of the road leading to Ramallah is still under the control of the Jewish state.[7] So, to repave the roads, they must obtain authoriza-

---

7. The Oslo process culminated in the signing in 1995 of the Interim Agreement on the West Bank and Gaza Strip by Israel and the PLO. Also known as the Taba Agreement or Oslo II, it divided the Palestinian territories into

First Moves

tion from the Israeli General Staff. My driver tempers my annoyance: it's not so bad today. When it rains, driving becomes almost impossible.

We pass UNRWA buildings[8] and schools, indicating the proximity of refugee camps. The condition of roads, buildings, and neighbourhood improve as we approach Ramallah. Much unsightly construction is underway, and approaching the city centre, traffic once again becomes difficult.

We finally arrived near the home of Karim, a journalist friend I had met in Cairo a few years earlier. He agreed to put me up during my short stay here. My cab pulls onto a traffic circle facing a building flanked by a Palestinian flag. The comically small building is the headquarters of the Palestinian Legislative Council. The image serves as a reminder: the Palestinians are, in numerical terms, a small people. The Council has not been in session for many months. Most of the parliamentarians, from Hamas, have been arrested by the Israeli government. My cab driver laughs at the situation: 'Inshallah, the Palestinian parliament is still meeting in prison!'

'Inshallah,' I reply, before leaving him.

---

three distinct zones: Zone A comprises the towns now administered by the Palestinian Authority; Zone B falls partially under Palestinian control, but the Israeli government continues to assume responsibility for security; and Zone C is under Israel's sole control. In 2000, on the eve of the outbreak of the second Intifada, the breakdown was as follows: Zone A: 17.2% of the total surface area of the occupied Palestinian territories; Zone B: 23.8%; Zone C: 59%.

8. UNRWA, established in 1949, is the United Nations Relief and Works Agency for Palestine Refugees in the Near East. UNRWA operates mainly in the Palestinian territories, Jordan, Syria, and Lebanon.

I check on Karim. He seems happy to have settled here and cover the conflict for various French media. I tell him about my plans: Tomorrow, I have my first appointment at Birzeit University. The following day, I'm received for interviews at the PLO's Negotiations Support Unit, a group of consultants who advise the Palestinian political leadership on their peace talks with the Israelis.

*

The Birzeit has a pleasant campus. Located a few kilometres from Ramallah, it is perched on a hill in a green and relatively unspoilt environment. The university enjoys a strong reputation. It partners with numerous American, European, and Arab institutions. Both foreign and Palestinian professors, most of them trained in the United States, teach here. Birzeit aims to be co-educational and secular. With its unions and associations, it functions as a good barometer of the prevailing political climate. In February 2000, Birzeit made a name for itself in France when it played host to Prime Minister Lionel Jospin, who was visiting the occupied territories at the time. The visitor had the misfortune to describe Hezbollah as a terrorist organization. He fled the campus as angered students pelted him with small stones.

On this sunny September day, students stroll around the campus. The young Palestinian bourgeoisie is all dressed up, often in the latest designer clothes. The female students, wearing light veils or uncovered hair, with their discreet but assertive charm, made an impression on me. Tight jeans and sunglasses are de rigueur. The atmosphere is light. At first glance, the place seems untouched by the horrors of the Occupation.

I was welcomed into the Faculty of Law where I presented my project to the dean, who speaks French. I tell him I'd be happy to teach law courses in English or French but that my level of Arabic is unfortunately insufficient to teach in that language. However, I remain confident that I can bring useful knowledge and experience to his students. There is no doubt in my mind that students at Birzeit, the flagship Palestinian university, are capable of learning in English. My interviewer, despite an obvious desire to be conciliatory, pouts. He doesn't think his students would be able to write papers in English. He says he'll take some time to consider my proposal. Seeing that the conversation isn't going very well, I thank him for his time and take my leave.

I return to Ramallah where I meet up with Karim and some of his friends. During our conversation, I learn that Dr Haidar Abdel Shafi has just passed away. A prominent Gazan physician, he was one of the leading figures of the Palestinian national movement, respected by the whole of Palestinian society, regardless of political affiliation. He was responsible for leading the first Palestinian delegation—Jordanian–Palestinian, to be exact—to sit down at the negotiating table with the Israelis. That was in 1991, at the Madrid Conference. Since then, the ranks of PLO leaders have thinned considerably. Israel's policy of liquidating Palestinian leaders, Arafat's manoeuvres to isolate his rivals, and old age have taken their toll on many of them. Today, however, everything is still up for negotiation.

*

The next day, I was received by the Negotiations Support Unit (or NSU) of the PLO's negotiations department. A tall, imposing Canadian man welcomes me. His slightly intimidating physique contrasts with his friendly welcome. He introduces me to the workings of this project—his own—which he launched almost 10 years ago. NSU is a branch of Adam Smith International (ASI). This British consultancy specializes in assistance with privatization and good governance. In the mid-1990s, in the wake of the Oslo Accords, ASI planned to offer its expertise in the economic development of the Palestinian territories. Faced with the lack of progress on the economic front, ASI quickly had to revise its plans. A few contacts within the PLO revealed a real need for legal and political expertise felt by the Palestinian leaders in charge of pursuing negotiations with Israel. The consultancy firm set about finding foreign-trained Palestinian professionals willing to lend their brains to the leadership in Ramallah. Thus, the NSU was born.

In 1999, what might have seemed an unlikely alliance was born: Adam Smith International, effigy of globalized capitalism, placed itself at the service of the PLO, the nationalist, the repentant "terrorist." To make matters worse, the British firm, with the help of the British Foreign Office and other European governments that provide financial backing for the NSU, was in a position to try and right the wrongs committed by the "perfidious Albion" and other European efforts in Palestine.

Today, the unit has over twenty employees: lawyers, political advisors, and a communications team. Palestinians from the Diaspora, some Palestinians from Israel trained at Israel's top universities, a few Jerusalemites, and Palestinians from the territories make up the bulk of the NSU.

I hear from the project manager that there are two vacancies for legal advisers: one on borders, the other on refugees. I'm invited to take part in three successive interviews in English. My interviewers are all in their thirties, and all very academically accomplished. The questions came thick and fast, technical, legal, and even eminently political. I was then presented with a case study on international law issues relating to the first Arab–Israeli conflict.

Following this battery of tests, I meet the project's main contact at the PLO, Mr Maen Areikat. A sedan awaits me. A driver accompanies me to the office of my host, the vice president of the PLO's Negotiations Affairs Department (NAD). I'm a little apprehensive, although this feeling is coupled with obvious curiosity—I've heard so many things, so much criticism of the PLO, its corruption, its incompetence, that I'm expecting the worst.

I step through Mr Areikat's door. An aesthetic sore hangs on his office wall. I find it hard to turn my attention away from this ugly painting, which achieves the feat of freezing the flow of a tropical waterfall. The man who welcomes me, however, is a pleasant surprise. Mr Maen Areikat makes quite an impression on me. He has a certain charisma and speaks fluent English. His speech is convincing, even if the interview is really just a long monologue on his part. He enjoys hearing his own voice. I'm asked just one question:

'Where's your family from?' My answer seems like a passkey: 'We're from Haifa, I'm from the Sanbar family.' His face opens in a smile. He stands up.

A little background is in order here. Before the Nakba,[9] Palestine was, like Lebanon, a country that could be described as quasi-feudal, controlled by a few 'big families.' To tell the truth, I've never quite understood what is meant by the term 'big family.' Nevertheless, the Sanbar family is one of those Palestinian families whose name evokes something here. It is also familiar to my interlocutor, since a cousin, Elias Sanbar, has long worked for the PLO in France. Now Palestine's representative to UNESCO, he is also renowned for his work on the history of Palestine and the question of refugees.

The interview finished, Maen walks me to the door. A warm tap on the shoulder punctuated the mention of my family. I have the impression that for him, it's all in the bag.

That evening, the project manager invites me to the annual NSU dinner. At the table, I meet most of the NSU employees and their spouses. There's an American–Lebanese–Palestinian, an American–Syrian, an Egyptian, Canadian–Palestinian, and Lebanese parentage, an Italian–Palestinian born in Dubai, Palestinians of Israeli nationality from the Galilee, and so on. This merry mix, an amiable and relaxed group, comes from the best international schools: Harvard, McGill, the London School of Economics, and Hebrew University, Jerusalem's main university.

---

9. An Arabic word meaning 'catastrophe,' it refers to the creation of the State of Israel and the Palestinian exodus of 1948. The Nakba is commemorated by Palestinians every May 15.

This dinner was also my first opportunity to meet Dr Saeb Erekat. He is the director of the NAD. He is often referred to as the PLO's *Chief Negotiator.*

'Dr Saeb,' as he's known, is a man with a very dull complexion. He's from Jericho. Of medium height, with a broad, balding forehead, he hides small, sharp, piercing eyes behind glasses. Since the Madrid conference, he has been involved in every round of negotiations. He caused a ruckus in the Spanish capital by proudly sporting a keffiyeh during the first meetings between the Jordanian–Palestinian delegation and the Israelis. At the time, the leader of the PLO, the 'terrorist' Yasser Arafat, was *persona non grata* in the peace talks. By donning this head covering, symbolizing the Palestinians' struggle for their land, Saeb Erekat affirmed his allegiance in the eyes of the world, with courage and determination. Since then, Saeb Erekat has become one of America's preferred interlocutors, earning the nickname 'Mr CNN' from Dennis Ross, President Bill Clinton's former Middle East envoy, for his penchant for media appearances. Now close to current PLO leader and President of the Palestinian Authority Mahmoud Abbas,[10] Saeb Erekat is a member of Fatah and Governor of Jericho. Along with Maen Areikat, he is the NSU's other main contact. They share the same surname but spell it differently—they're distant cousins.

Dr Saeb remains at the reception only briefly. It's just a chance for him to greet all the guests. I'm introduced

---

10. Mahmoud Abbas is more commonly known as 'Abu Mazen' (literally 'Mazen's father,' his eldest son) among Palestinians and in the Arab world. This second name is also used in the rest of the story.

by the other Areikat, who slips a few words into his ear. Saeb is smiling, obviously distracted by the good mood emanating from the gathering. We shake hands. He welcomes me. This short exchange gives me the impression, rightly or wrongly, that I'm already a member of the team. But I haven't signed anything yet; I haven't even been formally offered a job.

III

Beirut, Far From Annapolis
November / December 2007

The NSU is slow to give me an offer. At a time when the peace process between Israel and the PLO is resuming, this delay gives me time to think.

On 27 and 28 November 2007, a conference devoted to relaunching negotiations was held in Annapolis, Maryland, under the auspices of the US administration. The summit resulted in a handshake between PLO leader and Palestinian Authority President Mahmoud Abbas and Israeli Prime Minister Ehud Olmert. In a joint declaration, they agreed to begin immediate bilateral negotiations with a view to resolving the permanent status issues,[11] which should lead to the creation of a Palestinian state before the end of 2008.

Do I dare entertain that hope?

---

11. Permanent status issues were initially set out in the Declaration of Principles signed by Israel and the PLO on 13 September 1993. With a view to resolving the Israeli–Palestinian conflict once and for all, these agreements set a five-year deadline for settling the following issues: Jerusalem, refugees, settlements, security, borders and water: Jerusalem, refugees, settlements, security, borders, and water.

After the Madrid Conference in 1991 and the official meetings that followed in Washington, the Declaration of Principles signed by the PLO and Israel in 1993, the Jericho-Gaza Agreement of 1994, the Taba Agreement of 1995, the Wye Plantation Accords and the failed summits at Camp David in 2000 and Taba in 2001, it's hard to deny that in the Holy Land, the 'process' has long since taken precedence over 'peace.'

From the outset, therefore, I was sceptical about the Annapolis initiative. What's more, the Bush administration has a disastrous record in the Middle East. And George W. Bush has proved to be a loyal, constant, and unfailing ally of Ariel Sharon. Certainly, the support of the 'international community,' represented by some fifty nations at Annapolis, is real. But Iran and Hamas are MIA.

Yet the Arab Peace Initiative, which offers Israel regional normalization in exchange for withdrawal from the territories they've illegally occupied since 1967 and a just resolution of the refugee problem, is still on the table.[12] If Israelis and Palestinians reach agreement, it could offer a complete and lasting resolution to the Arab–Israeli conflict.

From the outside, this latest attempt to create a Palestinian state looked to be the last. Continued Israeli colonization of the West Bank and the weakening of the PLO, which has lost control of Gaza to Hamas, all bring uncertainty to the success of this effort. Ehud Olmert

---

12. Initially adopted in Beirut in April 2002, the peace initiative was signed by all Arab League member states, as well as by members of the Organization of the Islamic Conference. As such, Iran has also accepted the terms of this proposal.

made this statement to the press, which caught my eye: 'If one day the two-state solution collapses, and we have to face a struggle for equal voting rights like in South Africa (including Palestinians from the territories), then, as soon as that happens, the State of Israel will be finished.'

Since both sides want their own state, Israelis and Palestinians are running out of time.

The director of NSU finally sends me an offer. I had told him when we met that I was interested in the position on refugees. After much deliberation, I accept the offer: as of 15 January 2008, I'd be the NSU's—and therefore the PLO's—legal advisor on the refugee issue.

On reflection, given the current context, I don't believe there was a pursuit of serious negotiations. However, working on the technical development of the refugee dossier, acting in support of the promotion of their rights, was a prospect that motivated me. And despite all my reservations, I realized that this would be a unique opportunity to see things from the inside.

Nevertheless, I feel unable to commit myself to my new responsibilities without taking the pulse of the refugee camps. A few days later, before taking up my new post, I travel to Beirut for a short stay.

*

I've never felt totally at home in Lebanon. Apart from my imperfect command of the Arabic language, I've never felt that I belonged to this slightly mad people, with its eccentricities, attractions, and charms. Between my French identity and my attachment to the Palestinian cause, I've always felt that my link with this country was distant, even questionable. And yet, even though they haven't lived here for several decades, my mother, my uncles and my aunts identify as Levantines. They remain Lebanese citizens.

This is only the third time I've been to Beirut. The first was with my mother at the end of the civil war, in 1992, I think. I still remember Beirut as a ravaged ghost town, its houses and shops barely standing, the walls riddled with bullets. Strangely enough, this dilapidation held real beauty. The town, cut to the bone in places, was striking, as if magnetic. The Lebanese, always prospecting forward, were already starting to talk about reconstruction whilst arms continued to be widely used in the country. Syrian forces were still deployed in the country, and the Israeli army remained stationed in the south. Everything had to be rebuilt.

Ten years later, in 2001, during my second visit, the country had been radically transformed. Unrecognizable. Downtown Beirut had been largely rebuilt, the cranes were working., Lebanon was being rebuilt, and, despite crippling debt, the future looked bright. Southern Lebanon had just been liberated from Israeli occupation, allowing me to discover this magnificent region, its green hills still untouched by construction.

For the first time, I was also able to catch a glimpse of Israel, the Palestine of my grandparents. From the Lebanese border, where Hezbollah keeps a watchful eye,

I remember being moved by the neighbouring Galilee. I realized that my roots were somewhere here, on one side or the other of this front line. On both sides perhaps. But near the Mediterranean, yes, that's certain. For a brief moment, I found my place between the green hills, lulled by a gentle breeze, and the azure horizon. To my left, the sky-blue and white flag emblazoned with the Star of David fluttered. To my right, the yellow and green banner of the Party of God[13] torn by the wind, taunting its counterpart ostentatiously. Strangely enough, history, borders, conflict, and its madness had no hold on me at that precise moment. I was in familiar surroundings. I felt a sense of belonging.

I also remember being struck by those Israeli villages so close by, which, like clusters of pasteboard houses, sat so awkwardly into the landscape. The Lebanese Shiite movement presented itself as victorious in a war of attrition that had led to Israel's disengagement from the area. The foundations of Lebanon, this small country still under Israeli influence, remained tenuous. But a fresh wind was blowing again at the start of the new millennium. And the Lebanese were returning home, ever more numerous, ever more enthusiastic.

A few years later, the Cedar Revolution[14] initiated by the assassination of former Lebanese Prime Minister Rafik Hariri on 14 February 2005, confirmed this trend. I followed

---

13. *Hezbollah* means Party of God in Arabic.
14. The 'Cedar Revolution' was a movement that emerged in the wake of the assassination of former Lebanese Prime Minister Rafik Hariri, calling for the withdrawal of the Syrian army from Lebanon through large-scale demonstrations.

Beirut, Far From Annapolis

all this from a distance, but with interest—without understanding everything, of course, because Lebanese internal politics are indecipherable for the layman. But one thing seemed certain to me: civil society and young people had embarked on an implacable and hopeful change. As is so often the case in this country, for blessed and cursed alike, hope was abruptly to fade.

In the summer of 2006, Israel bombed and then invaded Lebanon. Once again. The Hebrew state wanted to permanently weaken Hezbollah, which was still active on the other side of the border, and put an end to the rocket attacks on its northern territory. I want to go there to help charter humanitarian aid. But Beirut, which was? no longer accessible by air, finds itself quickly cut off from the world. Damascus remained: I was about to buy a plane ticket to the Syrian capital when I learned that the road I wanted to take to reach Lebanon had been bombed. I watched the disaster from Paris, helpless. Lebanon had been set back 15 years.

*

This time, in these last days of 2007, Beirut becomes more familiar to me. I've booked a room in a hotel in Hamra, the district where my maternal family settled after the Nakba. I like it here. Here, Sunnis, Shiites, and Christians live side by side. My hotel is close to the church where my parents got married in August of 1975. Then, the Lebanese civil war was just breaking out.

The first day of my stay takes me to the Chatila refugee camp. Here, the memory of the massacres perpetrated on 16 and 17 September 1982 still lingers: with the implicit blessing of the Israeli army, then led by Ariel Sharon, several thousand Palestinian refugees[15] were murdered by Lebanese Phalangist militias in the Sabra and Chatila camps. I pause for a moment at a memorial erected to commemorate these deaths. It's a place that makes your blood run cold. The Palestinian martyrs, whose photos hang by the hundreds, look into your eyes and never fade. They touch your heart. They turn your stomach. Within this sanctuary, the trauma, the smell of death, always remains.

One of my uncles was UN representative in Lebanon at the time of the tragedy. Informed by a nurse, he was one of the first on the scene, where he opened the camp to journalists. I never managed to find out more; I never dared ask for more details. All I know is that he sent his telegram to UN headquarters in New York to report on the massacres. And that he was instructed to leave Beirut immediately, and to drive non-stop to Damascus. There, he was 'repatriated' to the United States, leaving behind him a Lebanon under the Israeli control, torn apart in turn, after the loss of the Palestine of his childhood. He flew to what became his adopted home: New York and the UN.

The Chatila camp is still there. I walk through it in the company of Roula[16] head of the main NGO working here. She's a smiling, dynamic woman in her forties. It's hard to

<hr>

15. Estimates of the number of victims of the Sabra and Chatila massacres vary from 700 (official Israeli figure) to 3,500.
16. This first name has been changed.

imagine how her life—devoted to improving the daily life of this dilapidated camp—hasn't diminished her joie de vivre. The camp remains a place apart, with its community life, its codes, and its shops.

We go to the house of one of the families living in Chatila. We are greeted by an elderly lady, almost sickly thin. Yet her facial features are still delicately delicate. She offers us coffee and chocolates from a carefully preserved box. Roula asks about her health and the family. I exchange a few words with her too. She's surprised by my broken Arabic, tinged with a strong Egyptian accent. I explain that I learned the language there. She smiles at me. I feel at ease, even if my presence seems to intrigue her a little. I tell her I'm off to Ramallah shortly, without going into details. Annapolis, the Bush administration's new resolutions, the Palestinian state—all this seems light years away from my hostess's daily life. I dread her reaction.

To tell the truth, our meeting, though stingy with words, is troubling me: what am I going to do in Ramallah? Wouldn't I be more useful here? In this house, I feel a little ashamed. Here, I don't fully accept my choice. The Palestinian Authority and its compromises probably don't get much press here, in the eyes of the refugees. Better to remain silent. It's hard to imagine that the PLO in Ramallah still represents the people of this camp, the Palestinians of Lebanon. They, who were the heart of the Palestinian resistance until the early 1980s, seem left to their own devices, forgotten by all.

The Palestinian woman keeps smiling at me. Her gaze remains locked on mine. She can't take her eyes off me either.

The old lady introduces me to her grandson, a big fellow in his thirties. Eissam has just woken,[17] a dark-haired man with very blue eyes and a porcelain complexion cut by a large scar on his chin. He has just washed up when he greets us warmly, his handshake firm and his gaze direct. He offers me a cigarette. Eissam works as a taxi driver and occasionally helps a friend who runs a garage. In Lebanon, many jobs are forbidden to Palestinians. Many work illegally to try and support themselves and their families.

The discussion continues. Despite an old stove that's past its prime, it's cold. They tell me about their village in Palestine, their broken family, their life here. I tell them about mine. At opposite ends of the world, our respective destinies couldn't be farther apart. But that's not the case—exile sometimes creates unexpected bridges. In this austere, empty room, time feels suspended, punctuated by assertive silences and smiles that are both modest and sincere. It's with regret that we must bring this meeting to an end. I approach our hostess to say goodbye. I find her beautiful. And I take Eissam's phone number.

We end our visit to Chatila with a detour to the NGO's offices. They're waiting for us there, but Roula is unable to tell me about the activities carried out by her organization, due to a power outage. They are a daily occurrence.

Over tea, Roula listens to visitors' grievances in her office. Chatila, already overcrowded, must cope with an influx of new refugees from the Nahr al-Bared camp. A few months ago, this camp was the scene of violent clashes between the

------

17. His first name has been changed.

Lebanese army and the radical Islamist movement Fatah al-Islam. Following the fighting, the Nahr al-Bared camp was razed by the army, resulting in the death of dozens of civilians and the forced departure of tens of thousands of Palestinian refugees.[18]

One by one, the day's visitors arrive. They all come from the destroyed camp. An old man with a keffiyeh is crying. I can hardly look at him. I think the desolation of the elders is the most disarming, their sadness the most inconsolable. They know it's too late to hope. Two little girls accompany him. They sit silently, their eyes wide open.

I understand that the NGO can do little to improve their lot. I stay until the last of these visitors is heard. I'd like to think it's out of politeness, out of respect for these people. The truth is, I'm glued to my seat, weighed down by the heaviness of the moment. Admiring, too, the work of these people of character, volunteers, who devote their lives to trying to ease their compatriots' misery. I feel very small in front of Roula's dedication. For her, this is just one day

---

18. Located near Tripoli in northern Lebanon, the Nahr al-Bared camp was founded in 1949 following the first Palestinian exodus. Until the end of May 2007, it housed around 31,000 refugees. On 20 May 2007, the camp was bombed by the Israeli army as part of reprisals against the extremist Fatah al-Islam faction. The Islamist group had previously killed 20 Lebanese soldiers, whose killers, who had taken refuge in the camp, refused to surrender. Initially, 10,000 refugees fled the fighting to other camps. On Sunday 15 July, for the first time in over 37 years, the Lebanese army decided to enter the camp. Violent clashes ensued. On Sunday, 2 September, the army announced that it had the camp under control. According to official figures, the fighting left at least 244 Palestinians dead (including 222 'activists') and 163 Lebanese army casualties. Some twenty Islamist fighters managed to escape. The camp itself was totally destroyed, emptied of its possessions and inhabitants.

among many. Just another day. Sixty years—it's been nearly sixty years since good souls have come to the aid of these exiles who have lost their homes, their homeland, who have often been separated from their families. Once, twice, sometimes more, each family carved up ad infinitum.

My day ends in a Raouché café by the sea, hookah in hand, the taste of coffee grounds in my mouth. Between life, surviving the camp and dozing off in front of the Mediterranean, a transition is perhaps missing. But my day had none. Lebanon doesn't know how to spare them. Images of Chatila are still running through my head. Only the contemplation of the setting sun, its reflections on the waves disappearing out to sea, brings me a touch of serenity. A few metres from me, a noisy table finishes what seems to be a long lunch. Four couples in their thirties are laughing and chatting. The women are all dressed up, lips deformed by Botox. Chatila is just a few kilometres from the revelry of the Beirut jetsetters. So goes Lebanon.

*

The next day, I take a cab to the UNRWA offices. My suspicious accent, long silhouette, thin beard, and dark suit convince my Shiite driver that I'm a brother from Tehran. Our trivial chat amuses me.

My meeting with the Director of UNRWA in Lebanon was less exhilarating. As UN officials are wont to do, he described the situation in the country's camps in technical, precise, almost sanitized, terms. His calm, measured tone contrasts with his description of the reality on the ground. It's catastrophic. Nahr al-Bared is naturally his main concern; some 30,000 Palestinian refugees are now lost in the wilds of Lebanon, with no roof over their heads, no home, and no means of subsistence. The fate of the other camps is no more reassuring. He advises me against visiting most of them. According to him, the situation is tense these days. He adds that UNRWA is not at its best financially. In short, the future of Palestinian refugees in Lebanon is worrying.

The corridors of the UN agency are decorated with photos illustrating the work carried out over the past sixty years. Some of the black-and-white shots date back to 1949–50, when the camps were little more than a succession of tents hastily erected to cope with the emergency of the Palestinians' forced exile. They disappeared with the return of the refugees.

'[R]efugees wishing to return to their homes and live at peace with their neighbours should be permitted to do so at the earliest practicable date...'

This is the wording of the famous Resolution 194, passed by the UN General Assembly on 11 December 1948. It embodies the famous 'right of return' of Palestinian refugees.[19] Over the past sixty years, however, the need to remedy

---

19. The right to return is enshrined in a number of international conventions. Among them, Article 13-2 of the 1948 Universal Declaration of Human Rights defines it as follows: 'Everyone has the right to leave any country, including his own, and to return to his country.' Article 12-4 of the 1966 International Covenant on Civil and Political Rights states: 'No one shall be denied the right to enter his own country.' Article 5 (d) (ii) of the 1965 International Convention on the Elimination of All Forms of Racial Dis-

the injustice initially committed has gradually taken a back seat to the new emergencies and priorities that the slow deterioration of the Israeli–Palestinian conflict generates daily. The tragic fate of Count Folke Bernadotte, the first UN-appointed mediator in the Arab–Israeli conflict, has been consigned to the dustbin of history, yet his warnings are still relevant today, and his itinerary remains illuminating.

The Scandinavian diplomat gained recognition at the end of the Second World War when he successfully organized a rescue operation for Norwegian, Danish, and French Jewish deportees. He saved 15,000 people from the hell of the Nazi concentration camps. Bernadotte was a good man.

On 20 June 1948, following the clashes over the partition of Palestine, Bernadotte was entrusted with the immense task of facilitating the cessation of fighting and overseeing the implementation of territorial division. On 16 September of that year, he submitted his recommendations to the Security Council. His conclusions were not made public until 20 September. His fate, however, was decided on the 17th: Bernadotte, accompanied by other UN employees, inspected various UN and Red Cross establishments in the Jewish sector of Jerusalem. The UN delegation's three vehicles were stopped by an Israeli jeep. Three men got out and sprayed the convoy with bullets. Bernadotte was gravely wounded and succumbed to his injuries.

---

crimination guarantees: 'The right of everyone, without distinction as to race, color, or national or ethnic origin, to equality before the law, notably in the enjoyment of the following rights [...] (d) (ii) The right to leave any country, including one's own, and to return to one's country.'

Beirut, Far From Annapolis

It's hard to forget the recommendations of the Swedish diplomat and his words about refugees:

'It would be an offence against elementary justice if these innocent victims of the conflict were denied the right to return to their homes while Jewish immigrants flock to Palestine and, in effect, threaten permanent replacement of Arab refugees who have been rooted in this land for centuries.'

To Bernadotte, 'No settlement can be just and complete without recognizing the right of Arab refugees to return to their homes.'

Between 1947 and 1949, over 726,000 Palestinians, both Christian and Muslim, became refugees after being expelled or fleeing the fighting that took place before and after the declaration of independence of the State of Israel.[20] During the 1967 war, more than 200,000 other Palestinians were forced to leave their homes in the West Bank and Gaza Strip (another 200,000, already displaced for the first time in 1947–1949, were forced into exile once again). Neither the 1948 refugees nor those displaced in 1967 have been authorized by Israel to return to their homes, which are now located either in Israel or in the occupied territories. Since then, expulsion measures targeting Palestinians

---

20. After decades of controversy, the work of Israel's 'new historians' has largely confirmed the Palestinian account of the causes of the Palestinian exodus. See for example: PAPPÉ (Ilan), *Le Nettoyage ethnique de la Palestine*, Paris, Fayard, 2008. Incidentally, it is important to note that the different readings of the events of 1947–1949 have no bearing on the validity of the right of return. In the eyes of the law, a person must be entitled to return to his or her home, whatever the reasons that may have motivated his or her departure.

in the territories have continued: revocation of residence permits, destruction of homes, confiscation of land.

In the course of this conflict, the temporary became permanent. In Israel, Jewish immigrants have replaced Palestinian refugees. Israel has built public gardens and state forests on the old stones of razed Palestinian villages. And UNRWA has become an institution, now in its sixties, operating in the West Bank, Gaza, Lebanon, Syria, and Jordan. Most refugees, now numbering almost 7 million[21] live less than 100 kilometres from the Israeli border. Tents have given way to camps, many of them built of concrete. Palestinians have not forgotten their original villages. In principle, these camps are always destined to disappear. Refugees still have the hope of returning home. It is their right.[22]

I forgot myself for a while in the corridors of the UNRWA offices. On the walls, more recent photos, this time in colour, show children playing in the camps. They were born there. Their eyes, large, black, sometimes blue or green, exude innocence. But the strength of these gazes calls out to me,

---

21. Palestinian refugees and their descendants make up the world's largest and oldest refugee population. It breaks down as follows: a) 4.5 million '1948 refugees' registered with UNRWA; b) 1.5 million '1948 refugees' who are not listed because they are never registered with UNRWA or because they were not in need of assistance when they became refugees; c) 950,000 people displaced as a result of the 1967 conflict.
22. The right to return is basically the right of the refugee to choose whether or not to return to his or her home country. The nature of this individual right makes it all the more difficult to negotiate, given that the Israeli government is opposed to the mass return of Palestinian refugees to territories now located in Israel and given that the personal choice of each refugee must be respected.

Beirut, Far From Annapolis

and I can't ignore their fate: *here, as everywhere, children play, they laugh, they cry. But where is their future? Is it in these camps that they will have to make their lives?*

*

This afternoon I'm meeting a friend in the port of Byblos, north of Beirut. I called Eissam to take me there. He meets me at the hotel reception, late. After a warm hug, he snatches the suitcases out of my hands. He refuses to let me carry a single bag. The hotel staff stare at us in a daze: Eissam's cowboy looks no doubt explain their surprise, though there's more to it than that. I can understand their reaction better when they see his car: a wreck. It would take a miracle for the antique Mercedes he uses as a vehicle to get us to our destination.

We set off. I'm happy to see Eissam again. So is he, apparently. He offers me a coffee. He insists. So we stop for a *kawa*, which we drink on the way. He insists on offering it to me—I have no say in the matter. So be it. My cappuccino is awful, but I force myself to drink it, so as not to offend him. His driving is slow and erratic at the same time. His car engine coughs out what's left of its lungs.

I need to go to the toilet. No sooner had we set off than we had to stop again. I already know I won't be on time for my appointment. Unfortunately, this stop is unavoidable, and Eissam is very proud to tell me that he knows the cleanest toilets in Beirut—I look at him, a little intrigued—he often washes in the *McDonald's* toilets. Embarrassed, I pretend to think it's normal. I nod. We'll stop at McDonald's, which is indeed clean. Less unsanitary than the Chatila refugee camp, that's for sure.

Back in the car, a wide-ranging discussion begins. Eissam has decided to tell me his life story. From then on, the cab ride became a slow-paced journey, in tune with his story. He speeds along the right-hand lane of the Lebanese *motorway* that runs along the coast, almost forgetting to look at the road, which makes me a little nervous.

Eissam's family came from a small village in Galilee, near Haifa. His parents were farmers. He has never known Palestine or Israel. Of Palestine, he knows only the camps in Lebanon, Chatila in particular. He was born there. About ten years ago, he obtained a visa for Denmark. He recalls his stay there with amusement. It was another world for him. He wanted to stay, but his visa was not renewed. After being noticed in a Copenhagen nightclub, he was arrested. He was sent back home to his camp. Since then, his life of adventure and odd jobs resumed.

'That's how it is,' he says. He doesn't seem to harbour any particular bitterness about his European experience. On the contrary, he has only good memories of it. The rest seems forgotten.

With a smile on his face, he tells me about an epic trip off the Danish coast. During a short summer holiday spent at the beach chasing girls, he decided to rent a boat with some visiting Palestinian friends. Eight of them spend the afternoon boozing under the sun in the small boat, before falling asleep, all of them absolutely plastered. Their painful awakening comes around sunset, with a chill in the air. The boat has drifted out to sea; the oars, fallen in the water, have been lost. The crew begins to panic. The friends on board can't swim. The coast is no longer visible on the horizon. Alerted by relatives on the beach, the local coastguard fortunately comes to the rescue of those buffoons. Eissam laughs heartily at his story. His laughter is infectious; I laugh too.

Our voices mask the noise of the engine, but don't make the Mercedes go any faster. Finally, I admit to him that I'm late. Big mistake: his face suddenly tenses up. His hands go to the steering wheel. His eyes leave my face. Eissam is now on a mission. The engine is ready to explode, my heart about to give out. Only the fact that he's finally looking at the road after driving blind for almost half an hour reassures me a little. Still, we're not going more than 70–80 kilometres per hour. Now that he's started, I don't have the heart to slow him down. Our fate is in God's hands.

A while later, we finally arrive at the port of Byblos. Safe and sound. I see my friend. Eissam helps me get the luggage out of the car. I take some money out of my pocket to pay him. He reacts violently: he refuses to let me pay him. I insist, but he doesn't give in. The argument escalates. The scene is surreal. He's ready to come to blows, but I'm desperate. What can I do? I have no choice but to thank him. We hug to the point of suffocation. I promise Eissam I'll be back soon.

*

I'm enjoying my last few days in Beirut, its restaurants, the evenings at Gemmayzeh, the trendiest neighbourhood in the city. I share a few moments, a little too brief, with a few friends. I no longer have any family here either. I find myself spending my last hours strolling the streets of the capital to the sound of Fairuz.[23] I listen to the voice of Lebanon on a loop. I'm enraptured, carried away by the lightness and power of her music, entranced by the singer's perfect phrasing. I let myself be carried away by the scents of this city of history, stories, and tragedies. The neighbourhoods still bear witness to the wounds of war and Lebanese rivalry. I am reminded of the writings of the poet Mahmoud Darwish[24] as well as accounts of the Lebanese war and the siege of Beirut in 1982.

After the Black September massacre[25] in 1970, the PLO was forced to leave Jordan for Lebanon. Driven into a new exodus after the siege of Beirut by the Israeli army in 1982, Arafat and his men left for Tunis. Many fell on the way. Most of the survivors of this generation are now in Ramallah. For some, it was a return to the Promised Land, but it was a new exile for many others.

---

23. Fairuz is one of Lebanon's most famous female singers.
24. Mahmoud Darwish (1941-2008), a world-famous poet, was also one of the most respected Palestinian figures. More than anyone else, he embodied the exile and dispossession of the Palestinian people, as well as their hopes of return.
25. 'Black September' is both the name of the massacre of Palestinians by the troops of King Hussein of Jordan in September 1970 and that of the organization created by Fatah, which carried out terrorist operations across the world in retaliation.

IV

RAMALLAH

JANUARY / FEBRUARY 2008

I decided to take up residence in Ramallah.

My first choice was East Jerusalem. As the announced capital of the future Palestinian state, it seemed only natural to live in the Holy City. A 'dead city,' I was told, controlled by the Israelis—depressing, to be avoided. The rent, the commute, and the uncertainty of crossing the Qalandia *checkpoint* every day convinced me: East Jerusalem as a capital is not on the immediate horizon. For the time being, I've given up, perhaps a little too quickly.

For many Palestinians, as for me, Ramallah is the default choice. This hilltop village with its many churches used to be a popular holiday resort in the region, thanks to its temperate climate. Since the Palestinian Authority moved there in the mid-1990s, the town has exploded. Located just a few kilometres—and a wall—from Jerusalem, Ramallah is now a bustling, congested, noisy city. The Christian petty bourgeoisie, now in the minority, mingles with a more numerous Muslim middle class. The local population is joined by the expatriate community, who live in a small area close to the city centre, dotted with a few bars and restaurants where people drink and dance.

By all accounts, Ramallah is a bubble within occupied Palestine. Here, at first, you don't feel the Israeli occupation—but you soon feel suffocated. You feel the need to escape from this cell. And as you leave the city, controlled by Palestinian Authority security forces, you're caught up by the occupation, the controls, the *checkpoints,* and the daily suffering that goes with them.

I moved into an apartment near the Qaddura refugee camp, five minutes from the city centre. The place doesn't look like much—even the decoration is in very bad taste. But it's a good compromise. Between the proximity of the refugees and that of the centre, I think I've found my place. I've identified the surrounding shops, the fresh juice vendor, the baker. I've found a gym where Ramallah's young bourgeoisie sweats to the sound of saccharine choruses and other barbaric remixes of the moment. The food served here is certainly not fancy, but two or three restaurants stand out from the crowd. And then I found a cleaning lady: Nahla.[26] A petite, energetic woman just over 1.50 metres tall, Nahla wears a light veil. She has a slight moustache. She cooks divinely well. My survival is assured.

*

My integration into the NSU feels natural. The negotiation process launched in Annapolis is in its infancy, and

---

26 .This first name has been changed.

the aim is to get me up and running as quickly as possible. At the start of 2008, the main concern for the Palestinian leadership in Ramallah is the continuing Israeli colonization of the occupied territories. On 5 December 2007, just over a week after pledging to pursue good-faith negotiations with the PLO in Annapolis, the Israeli Prime Minister announced the construction of 307 new housing units in Har Homa,[27] an Israeli settlement in East Jerusalem. The PLO was unable to obtain a freeze on Jewish construction in Palestinian territory, which Israel continues to pursue against all odds. Colonization, the illegal confiscation of new land, and the destruction of Palestinian homes will therefore continue, in parallel with the 'peace process.'

As the new round of negotiations gets underway, the NSU's young talent from all over the globe share many of the same fears. Perhaps the most significant worry is that the Palestinians will remain torn between Gaza and the West Bank, between Hamas and Fatah. The NSU leadership and its European backers see things very differently: after years spent preparing the dossiers, we're finally going to negotiate the permanent status of Palestine! Within the PLO, in Ramallah at least, the enthusiasm is quite similar. At Oslo, the PLO was committed to the logic of statebuilding. When the peace process stalled, followed by the second Intifada, the project remained at a standstill for many years. The Annapolis process is therefore the wagon not to be missed.

---

27. See map p. 94.

The PLO's challenge is gradually becoming clearer to me: to reach a peace agreement with Israel by the end of the year that can be accepted by the Palestinians in a referendum, enabling the creation of a viable and sovereign Palestinian state in Gaza and the West Bank soon. In this way, the Palestinian Authority hopes to regain the legitimacy of its people. In 2008, the PLO, which has lost control of Gaza, is playing for all it's worth.

On 17 December 2007, at a major donor conference in Paris, Salam Fayyad, the Palestinian Prime Minister, presented his vision of the future Palestinian state to his international partners:

Palestine is an independent, sovereign Arab state in the West Bank and Gaza Strip, determined by the 1967 border, with East Jerusalem as its capital. Palestine is a stable democratic state that respects human rights and guarantees equal rights and duties for all its citizens. Its people live in security in a safe environment subject to the rule of law, and it promotes equality between men and women. It is a state that values its social capital, cohesion and solidarity, and identifies with Palestinian Arab culture, humanist values and religious tolerance. It is a progressive state that values cordial relations with other peoples and states in the international community. The Palestinian government is open, inclusive, transparent and accountable. It is accountable to the needs of its citizens, provides basic services efficiently and enables the establishment of an environment conducive to the development of a prosperous private sector. Palestine's human resources are the driving force behind its national development. The Palestinian economy is open to other markets and aims to provide competitive, high value-added products and services, and in the long term, aspires to become a knowledge-based economy.[28]

A month later, Fayyad finally obtained $7.7 billion in pledges to complete the project, when the Palestinian Authority had only asked for $5.6 billion.

Do the Israelis share their goals?

While Ehud Olmert, like Ariel Sharon, has in the past declared his acceptance of the idea of a Palestinian state, it must be said that no Israeli leader or government has ever affirmed its commitment to the establishment of an 'independent and sovereign Palestinian state, on the 1967 borders, with East Jerusalem as its capital.'

From what I've seen since my arrival here, the Israeli military stranglehold shapes the Palestinians' past, present and future. Israel's outrageous violations of its international obligations dictate the reality of daily Palestinian life. The new peace process does little to change this—quite the contrary.

The other day, for once, I had two hours to kill. I started reading an NSU report on Israeli violations of the Road Map[29] since the Annapolis summit—in other words, since

---

28. Presentation taken from the Palestinian Authority document dated 17 December 2007, 'Building a Palestinian State: Towards Peace and Prosperity.'
29. The 'Road Map' is a Bush administration initiative endorsed by the Quartet (UN, EU, USA, Russia) on 30 April 2003. Its aim is to bring about a phased settlement of the Israeli–Palestinian conflict, based on the coexistence of two states. It includes clear stages, a timetable and criteria designed to encourage progress through reciprocal measures by both parties in the political and economic fields, as well as in the development of Palestinian institutions.

Ramallah

the parties' commitment to negotiate in good faith, in accordance with their international obligations. I couldn't believe my eyes.[30] It took the wind out of my sails: does it make sense to remind people of the law when you know that violating it will not be punished? It's a question worth asking. After a while, you tend to forget the law. Even me, a lawyer.

---

30 The figures presented in the report cover the period from 27 November 2007 to 27 January 2008. As part of the Road Map, the Israeli government committed to freezing all settlement activity in the West Bank - including East Jerusalem and the natural growth of settlements. Announced in early December, the tender for the construction of 307 new housing units in Har Homa was confirmed by the Israel Land Administration (ILA). Since then, a new project for the construction of several hotels and houses in the Gilo settlement, north of Bethlehem, has been validated, and a new call for tenders for 440 housing units in East Talpiot, south of Jerusalem's Old City, near the Palestinian village of Sur Baher, has been endorsed. Meanwhile, outside occupied East Jerusalem, 2,500 housing units were under construction in the West Bank in the third quarter of 2007, according to the Israeli Central Bureau of Statistics. Another Israeli obligation is the immediate dismantling of *outposts* established since March 2001. Since the Annapolis summit, only 2 of the 110 outposts have been dismantled. The Israeli government undertook to reopen Palestinian institutions in East Jerusalem. To date, the ten Palestinian institutions closed on 8 August 2001 remain closed, including the Palestinian Chamber of Commerce and Orient House. Finally, the Israeli government had agreed not to take any measures undermining confidence between the two parties, such as deportations or attacks on civilians; confiscation or demolition of Palestinian homes and property, as a punitive measure or to enable Israeli construction; destruction of Palestinian institutions or infrastructure. Since 27 November 2007, incursions, destruction, assassinations, arrests and other attacks on Palestinians and their property have multiplied: Israel has killed 165 Palestinians and wounded 521. Meanwhile, Israel also arrested 965 Palestinians (including 63 children) in the West Bank and Gaza. These are in addition to the 11,500 political prisoners already held in Israeli jails. The Israeli army continues to act unilaterally in areas under the control of the Palestinian Authority, as witnessed by recent incursions into the city of Nablus. In fact, the Israeli army is expanding its military presence in the West Bank each day. As of 11 December 2007, 561 *checkpoints* and other roadblocks prevent the free movement of Palestinians in the West Bank, an increase of 50 per cent since August 2005.

What I can't get over, however, is all the violence the Palestinians are still enduring after forty years of occupation, almost sixty years after the Nakba. I confess, after just a few weeks here, I can't imagine how these people are still surviving, physically and mentally. I think the day-to-day life of the territories is catching up with me. Already.

*

My life here naturally differs from that of a Palestinian in the West Bank[31] For at least three reasons: firstly, I'm French, which, all things considered, greatly facilitates my movements within the West Bank, between the West Bank and Israel, and outside their borders. Second, I work as an advisor to the PLO in negotiations with Israel, which generally gives me a few privileges, but also occasionally justifies more stringent control measures. Finally, my income is much higher than that of the Palestinians, most of whom live below the poverty line.

On the occasion of my first steps in the territories, however, I have resolved to try to 'live like a Palestinian.' I want to develop an enlightened judgment, fully aware of the living conditions of the people here. So, in these first few weeks in Ramallah, I'm sticking to a few simple rules: eat Palestinian, for example, whenever possible, and only use *checkpoints* open to locals. The first rule leads me to

---

31. Palestinians in East Jerusalem enjoy separate status and are considered residents of the municipality. As a result of the blockade and the Hamas boycott, Palestinians in Gaza live in even poorer conditions, with virtually no freedom to leave the territory.

Ramallah

eat mainly market produce and to refuse to buy products exported to the territories by the Israeli occupiers. To be fair, my frequent restaurant meals betray a definite departure from this principle, since I doubt that restaurateurs are as careful as I am about the origin of their products. The second rule obliges me to pass through the Qalandia *checkpoint* when coming and going between Ramallah and Jerusalem.

Arriving from Ramallah at the *checkpoint*, we pass through two refugee camps: Al Amari and Qalandia[32] I would later learn that many of the people living in these camps come from the town of Lod[33] Located a few dozen kilometres from here, near Ben Gurion airport in Israel, Lod is served by Highway 1, which links Jerusalem to Tel Aviv. The town was built on the remains of the Palestinian village of Lydda. An Arab community still lives there, on the other side of the wall. These Palestinians are Israeli citizens.

Coming from Ramallah, the road just skirts the camps. We don't stop there. But the local youngsters rarely miss the opportunity to profit at the *checkpoint*. The congestion of cars awaiting inspection creates a captive clientele, quickly assailed by beggars, chewing-gum sellers, and window wipers. My rental car is easily identifiable, so I'm systematically subjected to the heckling of the camp children, always whining, sometimes aggressive.

In fact, it's not just young people who live near the Israeli checkpoint. On a recent visit, I was taken to task by an old

---

32. See map p. 94.
33. See map p. 225.

man wearing a keffiyeh and traditional dress. The old man insisted on washing my car windows. Despite a polite but firm refusal on my part, reiterated afterwards by honking my horn, the episode almost turned ugly. The old man didn't comply. I refused to pay him. The outcome: a spit on my windscreen, a kick in my car door, and that hateful look which, for a moment, made my blood run cold.

Often, Israeli soldiers don't care about these slices of Palestinian life. They inevitably repeat themselves before their very eyes, as they wait, the drivers become irritated, and their troublemakers get in the way. The violence is exacerbated as we approach the *checkpoint*. Occasionally, however, these sketches become a source of mockery for the young soldiers of the Hebrew state. One day, when I persisted in refusing to have the windows of my car washed, two kids, in retaliation, amused themselves by attaching an empty Coke can to my rear windscreen. I didn't realize it until I got in front of the soldiers. The boys had already fled, laughing their heads off. The soldiers were laughing too.

I've since realized that I have no choice but to pay five shekels every time a poor child is a little too insistent. Every time I pass through Qalandia, I pay this tax to get through the tollbooth unhindered. My windows, regularly washed in brackish water, get dirtier by the day.

As you can imagine, the leadup to Qalandia is often more hectic than reaching the infamous *checkpoint*. After trying in vain for long minutes to manoeuvre past vehicles better positioned in the queue, the drivers finally resign themselves to lining up in two lanes. They come to a halt in front of the first Israeli checkpoint, which is completely opaque. From this booth, protected from all contact with the Palestinians, comes a woman's voice, barking at the drivers in Hebrew. I don't understand Hebrew. I just hear this shrill, aggressive voice ripping through an old microphone. She shouts her orders: 'Wait! Then: 'Move!' Or so I imagine—I usually manage by following the flow of cars to the second stop.

At the second stop, depending on the day, two or three lines are open to cars. We're usually welcomed by a pair of soldiers. *Welcomed* is a generous term. I don't know if a*waited* would even be appropriate. It's all very mechanical. Few soldiers deign to open their mouths—there's no need. The ritual is perfectly familiar to Palestinians: presentation of identity papers, then opening of the trunk.

The young soldiers, engulfed in their enormous bulletproof vests and laden by their intimidating rifles, control and inspect. Some of them glare at us. But more often than not, their attitude betrays an obvious indifference that I find hard to discern whether it's the expression of an assumed sense of superiority or a certain form of resignation. Sometimes, the eyes of these teenagers betray fear. As for the Palestinians, they comply, usually without flinching. As the rotation goes by—and the vagaries of an ever-bigoted Jewish immigration—we bend to the commands of a pretty Ethiopian girl who has trouble making herself understood; a tall, pimply, young Russian who puffs out his chest; or a dark-eyed Sephardic girl who might look Palestinian if she didn't take great pleasure in giving her Arab 'brothers' a hard time.

This is what a *checkpoint* looks like. They abound here.[34] All the same, all different. They have become the daily life of the Palestinians. They have become Palestine. They have even become part of its identity, that of a people surviving the course of history, but forced to bend its back. As proof of this, the *checkpoint* has recently become a fashionable artistic subject, particularly in films, giving rise to fantastical digressions and ecstatic sequence shots.

The Palestinian Authority has never been able to obtain the closure of a single checkpoints. After all, the Israeli General Staff administers the occupation, opens, moves, and rearranges *checkpoints,* as it sees fit. More rarely, it closes one or two. The Sulta[35] has no say in the matter; the 'Authority' has nothing to do with it—authority without power, then. An authority that hopes, by the end of the year, that Israel will have agreed to return East Jerusalem to it. An authority that hopes, by the end of the year, that Israel will be lenient enough to recognize something resembling the right of return for Palestinian refugees.

How can it be? Perhaps this is the ultimate expression of the Palestinians' disarray? Unless we can only survive by hoping, again and again, more and more, as everything deteriorates. As the territories imprison, the spirit discovers new horizons each time. Darwish, the poet, sees hope as a

---

34. OCHA, the UN organization for the coordination of humanitarian affairs in the occupied territories, counted 576 *checkpoints* and other obstacles to freedom of movement in the West Bank at the beginning of 2008. For up-to-date information on the humanitarian situation in the territories: http://www.ochaopt.org
35. The Palestinian Authority is called 'Sulta Falestiniya' in Arabic.

disease. A Palestinian disease par excellence, it is the ultimate remedy for the occupation:[36]

The occupation not only deprives us of the basic conditions of freedom, it goes so far as to deprive us of the very essentials of a dignified human life, declaring permanent war on our bodies and dreams, on people, houses, trees, committing war crimes. It promises us nothing better than apartheid and the ability of the sword to conquer the soul.

But we suffer from an incurable disease called hope. Hope for liberation and independence. Hope for a normal life in which we are neither heroes nor victims. Hope that our children will go safely to school. Hope that a pregnant woman will give birth to a living baby in a hospital, and not a dead child in front of a military checkpoint. Hope that our poets will see the beauty of the colour red in roses rather than in blood. Hope that this land will regain its original name: land of love and peace.

*

After Haidar Abdel Shafi died in September 2007, George Habash passed away in January 2008. At the age of 82, the emblematic figure of the Popular Front for the Liberation of Palestine (PFLP) succumbed to heart disease.

From a Christian Palestinian family, Habash was born in Lydda in 1926. He and his family were expelled from their

---

36. Speech delivered on 25 March 2002 to writers who had come to express their support for the Palestinian people in Ramallah, then under siege by the Israeli army.

hometown in July 1948. As you may recall, Lydda was wiped off the map in favour of Lod, Israel. George Habash found refuge in Beirut and studied medicine at the American University of Beirut (AUB). He founded the PFLP after the 1967 war, on the rubble of Nasser's Arab nationalism. From then on, the PFLP amplified the actions carried out by its *fedayeen*[37] from Jordan and made a name for itself by hijacking planes. It would later oppose the PLO's new orientation and the idea of a Palestinian mini-state in the West Bank and Gaza. Habash was one of the most ardent opponents of the Oslo Accords.

Some 15 years later, Mahmoud Abbas, the forgotten architect of the agreements,[38] does not hold this against him. In an official speech, the head of the PLO and president of the Palestinian Authority paid tribute to this 'great patriot.' An official three-day mourning period was ordered. For Abu Mazen, 'The death of this historic leader is a great loss for the Palestinian cause and for the Palestinian people for whom he fought for sixty years.'

Outside the territories, Abbas's communication caused an uproar: the PLO, the repentant negotiator, got caught up in its own history. Despite its willingness to fall into

---

37. *Fedayeen* means in Arabic 'those who sacrifice themselves for something or someone.' These Palestinian commandos emerged following the Arab defeat of 1967. They made repeated incursions into Israel from Jordan until the fighting of September 1970 (Black September), following which the PLO and the main Palestinian struggle movements were largely ousted from the Hashemite Kingdom.

38. Following the Oslo Accords, the Nobel Peace Prize was awarded in 1994 to Yitzhak Rabin and Shimon Peres on the Israeli side, and Yasser Arafat on the Palestinian side. Mahmoud Abbas, whose role was central to the initiation and conclusion of these agreements, was not awarded the prize.

line, the PLO remains, for international opinion, in the collective unconscious, a movement that used international terrorism to achieve its ends, which were, moreover, unsuccessful. Its image still suffers.

Worse still, among its own people, the PLO's popularity has reached hitherto unexplored depths over the last twenty years. For most Palestinians, the PLO was guilty of signing the Oslo Accords. Fifteen years after these agreements, decried by Edward Said[39] and most of the Palestinian intelligentsia, the logic has proved its limits: colonization has accelerated, the Intifada resumed, and the occupation hardened.

Institutions and a draft government have certainly been put in place, but these are largely dependent on the wishes of Israel and the international community. How could it be otherwise? What Israel occupies, the international community finances. In the few autonomous Palestinian territories, it is Mahmoud Abbas' Authority that is responsible for neutralizing Palestinians suspected of endangering Israel's security. The country may still be occupied, but any Palestinian act of violence must be suppressed. This is the job of the Sulta, nicknamed *Salata, or 'salad' in* Arabic.

The situation was further aggravated by the victory of Hamas in the Palestinian legislative elections in 2006. The result of the election is indisputable. In fact, it was approved by all the international observers responsible for ensuring

---

39. Edward Said (1935–2003) was the Palestinian intellectual par excellence until his death in 2003. Born in Jerusalem and now an American citizen, he was a professor of comparative literature and a musicologist. He is notably the author of *Orientalism,* considered one of the founding texts of postcolonial studies, as well as numerous writings on the Israeli–Palestinian conflict.

that the elections ran smoothly. But Hamas is a threat to Israel. As Ismail Haniyeh[40] was appointed to form the new Palestinian Authority cabinet, Ehud Olmert, acting Israeli Prime Minister, declared: 'We will not negotiate or deal with a Palestinian Authority dominated in whole or in part by an armed terrorist organization calling for the destruction of the State of Israel.' The Americans and Europeans followed suit: they refused to see Hamas as the representative of the Palestinian people. International subsidies were blocked, Israeli attacks increased, as did clashes between Fatah and Hamas. On 15 June 2007, tensions reached a climax when Hamas forces took control of the Gaza Strip, completely ousting Fatah from the territory. On 17 June, Mahmoud Abbas dismissed Ismail Haniyeh as Prime Minister. In his place, he appointed former Finance Minister Salam Fayyad, a former senior World Bank official popular with the Americans. Since then, the Ramallah-based government has controlled only the few territories in the West Bank that Israel has agreed to let it control.

To this day, officially, Israel, the US and the EU—the first apologists for democracy in the Middle East—persist in only dealing with the PLO and Sulta. This does not prevent the Israelis and their allies from questioning the ability of their Palestinian partner to represent all its people and to ensure the implementation of agreements already reached and yet to be reached. '*Sulta, Salata,*' it's really a load of rubbish they're telling us.

---

40. Born in 1962 in Gaza, Ismail Haniyeh is a Hamas politician. He was Prime Minister of the Palestinian Authority from 21 February 2006 to 14 June 2007.

V
GAZA, THE WARNING SHOT
JANUARY / FEBRUARY 2008

On 17 and 18 January 2008, Israeli military incursions left around twenty people dead in the Gaza Strip. According to the hackneyed official version, the aim of the operations was to put an end to the launching of rockets into southern Israel.

A few days later, Gazans detonated a section of the wall separating Gaza from Egypt. The border collapsed, leading to a massive but brief exodus of tens of thousands of Palestinians. Gaza is barely 100 kilometres from Ramallah. But I can't get there, and it's through Al Jazeera that I witness the pouring into the Egyptian desert of this martyred people, who are finally able to breathe. Subjected for many months to an extremely severe blockade, the Gazans are taking advantage of this unique opportunity to replenish their supplies in neighbouring Egypt.

On 20 January, Gaza's only power station gave out. Suddenly, 800,000 Palestinians were plunged into darkness. Gaza survives by candlelight.

In Ramallah, solidarity rallies are multiplying. I'm taking part. Like everyone else, I'm shaken by the events. In the evening, with great dignity, together, in silence, a few hundred Ramallahites meditate, under the watchful eye of the Palestinian security forces present in large numbers. Some soldiers are offered candles. The bare faces of the young demonstrators and the moustachioed faces of the Authority policemen, simply lit by the ephemeral flame of these candelabras, are a beautiful sight.

Unfortunately, contact between the West Bank and Gaza is becoming increasingly rare. I'm condemned to follow Gaza's slow agony from a distance; on television, but also thanks to the news brought back here and there by foreign journalists and humanitarians who can still get there. I, despite my French nationality, cannot go to Gaza without special authorization. So Gaza and its often-surreal stories are relayed to me. I'm on the lookout for the slightest piece of news from the Palestine we've been cut off from. I understand that there, the heart of the Palestinian resistance beats, in Gaza.

As far as politics are concerned, the fate of the small Mediterranean strip of land and its people is back in the spotlight. These painful events will, I hope, be a blessing in disguise. Further negotiations with the Israelis no longer seem to be on the agenda in Ramallah. With the city in mourning, the PLO, even if it wanted to, could not afford to resume talks. In a youthful, peaceful atmosphere, to the sound of bells and Palestinian nationalist songs, a demonstration of a few thousand Ramallahites led us to the Mukataa, the headquarters of Mahmoud Abbas' Authority.

I sang, 'One, one nation,' for national reconciliation; 'With spirit, with blood, I am with you, Gaza,' with my friends, including some from the NSU. In homage to these Gazan brothers who I don't know.

*

Faced with the tragic fate of Gaza, I'm reminded of the words of an Israeli friend: 'Gaza is free from Israeli occupation. With all the money invested in Gaza since the withdrawal of Israeli forces, the Palestinians could have turned it into a new Hong Kong. Instead, they chose violence and Hamas.'

Let's set the record straight: the Gaza Strip is not free of the Israeli yoke. Israel still controls all access points. Neither yesterday nor today is Gaza positioned to become a new Hong Kong. Over the course of exile and confrontation, this small piece of land has become a last refuge, a trapdoor rather, where an exsanguinated population—of mainly refugees—is holed up, denied the right to return home. Gaza remains rebellious, demanding, and violent. It suffers from a thousand ills. Today, it is ostracized. The closure of the Gaza Strip, first in small doses in 1992 and reinforced at the start of the second Intifada, has become systematic since June 2007, when Hamas took control of the territory. With Israel and Egypt locking their respective border crossings, products and people can only enter and leave sporadically.

More than ever, this overpopulated, impoverished scrap of land wedged between Egypt and Israel has become an open-air prison.[41] The Gaza Strip has been in a state of humanitarian crisis since April 2006, when the closure of the borders and the block of humanitarian aid caused a severe shortage of petrol, medical aid, and certain food-stuffs. Since then, Gazans have been suffering from a flagrant lack of basic necessities, and rising prices have prevented families from eating properly. In January 2008, only the most urgent medical cases and a few hand-picked international organizations are allowed through the Erez crossing into the territory. Medicines enter only in dribs and drabs. Due to the lack of petrol, power cuts occur frequently in the Gaza Strip's main hospitals. In a state of emergency, they now only accept the most extreme cases.

*

Abbas sent a letter to the Quartet representatives. In it, the President of the Palestinian Authority describes developments in the territories since the Annapolis summit: a new wave of settlements launched just a few days after the conference, and Gaza was attacked the day after the first official day of negotiations. He writes:

These actions not only violate the commitments made under the Roadmap, erode the Palestinians' faith in the peace process and their trust in the Israelis' sincerity and desire for peace, but also constitute violations of the

---

41. To date, only two access points to Gaza remain: Erez, on the Israeli side, and Rafah, on the Egyptian side. These border crossings are generally closed, unless special authorization is granted extremely sparingly by the Israeli and Egyptian authorities.

Palestinians' most basic rights under international law [...] I still believe that the Annapolis process is the best chance for peace we've had in years. Peace is the noblest of goals, and neither the Israelis nor the Palestinians nor the international community can afford to lose this opportunity, which could be our last.

A few days later, as Israeli military operations intensified in Gaza, Saeb Erekat hardened his tone, stating that 'negotiations with Israel are impossible as long as the Israeli army continues its raids on the Gaza Strip.' The decision to suspend meetings with the Israelis followed shortly afterwards.

On 24 January 2008, Mahmoud Abbas and Ehud Olmert met to discuss matters, but their agenda consisted of four letters: Gaza.

*

Officially, the PLO broke off negotiations in response to Israeli military operations in Gaza. Hopefully, this will provide the opportunity for a genuine attempt at national reconciliation between Hamas and Fatah. As January draws to a close, I'm heading to work with a slightly calmer mind. It may sound strange, I know, but I had anticipated that these peace talks would fizzle out. Now that the negotiations have been suspended, I'll be able to get to grips with the refugee issue for which I'm responsible.

At the office, as I'm dozing off reading one of our studies, a new message, marked 'confidential,' appears on my computer screen. Intrigued, I rush to open it. Two attachments are attached to the e-mail. They are entitled 'Meeting minutes 22 1 08' and 'Meeting minutes 27 1 08.'

The truth suddenly dawns on me, without pretence this time: negotiations were never interrupted, despite the events in Gaza and the apparent emotion shown by the PLO. In the greatest secrecy, Palestinians and Israelis met last 22 January then again on 27 January, each time in West Jerusalem hotels. Eager to find out what was said while the Palestinians of Gaza were left to the mercy of the IDF, I went through the minutes of these meetings page by page. For the first time, I've had the incredible opportunity to find out what was really going on. I now have access to the hidden negotiations, the 'peace process.'

On 22 January, Saeb Erekat and Abu Alaa[42] former Prime Minister and leader of the new Palestinian negotiating delegation, met with Tzipi Livni, Israel's Foreign Minister, and Tal Becker, her Chief of Staff. At this meeting, the parties agreed to set up the general structure necessary for the negotiations to run smoothly. At the same time, they agreed to hold discussions on borders and security. Refugees were also raised by Livni, who made her thoughts clear:

For the refugees, quite frankly, the Israeli position is that the creation of the Palestinian state is the answer to the problem. [...] I don't want to disappoint anyone, but no Israeli official, whether from the Knesset or the government, nor the public, will support the return of refugees to Israel. There are many people in the world who are willing

---

42. Like Mahmoud Abbas (Abu Mazen), former Prime Minister Ahmed Qoreï is more often referred to as Abu Alaa, after his eldest son.

to help on the refugee issue, and I'm not talking about Saudi Arabia but Bill Gates and his peers.

Livni's logic is deceptively simple. The slogan of the Annapolis process is unambiguous: 'two states for two peoples.' Within this framework, Palestinian refugees are destined to live in the future Palestine.

Abu Alaa reiterates the PLO's position: 'The right of return and compensation for refugees who decide not to return home, in accordance with UN General Assembly Resolution 194.' He asks Saeb Erekat to start working on the issue. His Israeli contact will be Tal Becker. The discussion continued with the Palestinians raising the question of Jerusalem. Livni was careful not to reveal her position. She remains silent.

Gaza only enters the discussion at the very end of the meeting. There's no hint of aggression, or even bitterness, in the words of the PLO leaders. On the contrary, they're only thinking about the gamble they've committed themselves to so wholeheartedly: concluding a peace agreement with the Israelis. The reality is that they are also at war with Hamas. Abu Alaa's speech is straightforward:

'We will defeat Hamas if we reach an agreement, and this will be our answer to their claim that recovering our land can only be done through resistance.'

Saeb Erekat is in the same frame of mind. He challenges the Israelis: 'Give me a fair deal and you'll have the support of 80 per cent of Palestinians.'

On 27 January, at a new meeting in Jerusalem, the Palestinian delegation briefly returned to reality. Abu Alaa tries to call them to order:

Gaza, the Warning Shot

Before we can begin serious talks, we must clear the table of all violations and obstacles to progress in negotiations, without exception, especially the siege, incursions, assassinations, murders and arrests in the West Bank and Gaza. The blockade recently imposed on Gaza and the shortage of petrol and basic necessities are very serious facts which cannot be accepted or neglected. [...] Under no conditions can we accept the continuation of settlement activity in the occupied West Bank, including East Jerusalem [...] We cannot continue to negotiate in the light of Israeli policies and violations. [...] It makes no sense to negotiate issues whose future Israel has already determined by imposing new realities on the ground. We will never accept the construction of the wall, the expansion of settlements, the maintenance of wilderness settlements and the continued closure of Jerusalem's institutions.

The diatribe elicited no reaction from the Israeli side; Livni didn't even deign to reply. So, the 'serious' discussions on borders and security begin. The Palestinians point out that they cannot accept anything less than the 1967 Green Line. They added that any modification, any exchange of territory could only take place on an equal basis.[43] Livni doesn't care. For her, the 1967 borders, the green line 'is not sacred.' Her approach is security-oriented. She wants to

---

43. After the 'historic compromise' of the 1988 Algiers Declaration, in which the PLO agreed to create a state on only 22 per cent of Mandate Palestine, this represents a further weakening of Palestinian positions. During the Camp David and Taba rounds of negotiations, the Palestinian delegations had never officially accepted the principle of land swaps, which were supposed to accommodate the Jewish settlements illegally established on Palestinian territory.

protect her state and her people. To this end, she specifies that the Palestinian state must be completely demilitarized.

At first glance, the gaps between the positions of the two parties seem like an abyss. But that's no surprise—discussions have only just begun. Nothing must be compromised, and everyone is aware of the difficulties that stand in the way of peace. The challenge remains immense.

At this meeting on 27 January, Dr. Saeb enthused: 'Whoever is able to reach an agreement to resolve this conflict, he will become the most important figure in the region since Jesus Christ!'

VI
'Palestitanic'
February / March 2008

Bernard Kouchner is visiting the Palestinian territories.

The NSU was asked to give a presentation of the PLO positions being discussed in negotiations with the Israelis. The date is 17 February 2008. The meeting was held at *Darna*, Ramallah's premier restaurant. The French delegation arrives in numbers, but without Kouchner, who seems to have been delayed. Among the members of the mission, I recognize Elisabeth Guigou, the former Socialist minister. Intrigued by her presence, I question one of the French security officers. 'She's the Minister's personal guest,' replies the man in the earpiece. The meeting begins, without the Minister.

Kouchner, the French Foreign Minister, arrives about ten minutes later, exasperated and exhausted by his day of meetings. The *French doctor* wants some fresh air and to go for a walk. He takes Maen Areikat, our team chairman, under his arm and asks Areikat to accompany him outside for a chat. We all look at each other, dumbfounded. The NSU presentation continues without them.

As luck would have it, the Minister comes back into the room just as I'm about to talk about refugees. I'm pleasantly surprised by his attentiveness. We tackle the question of compensation for refugees. I remind him that compensation should only be considered when the restitution of property confiscated by Israel nearly sixty years ago is no longer possible. I explain the different types of loss we have identified and evaluated. We quickly discuss the amounts that would solve the problem. He puts forward some uncertain figures from an Israeli–Palestinian think-tank financed by France: the Aix Group. This project indicates that with a few tens of billions of dollars, the whole issue could be resolved. I explain to him that the evaluation techniques adopted by this very superficial study are unsatisfactory. He says, emphatically, 'You Palestinians are historically right, but you're economically wrong!' I don't understand what he means. His delegation nods, smiling.

As the conversation progresses, I understand that France, which takes over the presidency of the European Union in July, is trying to get its nose into the Israeli–Palestinian talks. Kouchner proposes that France host one of the negotiating committees currently being set up. One of my colleagues deftly takes advantage of a moment of silence to bring to the table an issue that is far more burning in our eyes: the ongoing construction of the Jerusalem tramway by the French companies Veolia and Alstom. The tramway's route cuts through occupied Palestinian territory. The project is in response to a call for tenders issued by the Israeli government to build a streetcar line linking Jerusalem to Jewish settlements on the West Bank. The head

There Will Be No Palestinian State

of French diplomacy responds with a shrug. He admits that it is indeed a problem, but seems powerless, or reluctant, to commit.

The meeting comes to an end. One of the French diplomats, visibly pleased with the meeting, says with a smile: 'Bravo! Best of luck, hang in there!' I don't know how to interpret this encouragement. Perhaps they sum up the position of French diplomacy towards the Palestinians. For my part, I feel I've taken part in a pleasant, but inconsequential, attraction.

*

It's very cold in Ramallah; snow was falling heavily. For several days, shops remained closed. The city was paralyzed, and everyone stayed at home. But like many Ramallah residents, I had heating problems even though my gas bills are exorbitant. On my landlord's advice, I bought a *souba*, a small stove that follows me around the house as I move. I can't wait for winter to be over.

Salam Fayyad announces that he no longer believed in the possibility of an agreement in 2008. He sees two obstacles: continued settlement activity and military incursions into the West Bank. He forgets Gaza. In the Israeli ranks, it is also believed that a peace treaty before the end of 2008 is out of reach. For Deputy Prime Minister Haim Ramon, the signing of a declaration of principles before the end of 2008 would be a more reasonable objective. In his view, the objective now must be to produce a document that is sufficiently detailed to set in motion a program that would enable the establishment of a Palestinian state within two or three years. His vision of the future of the Gaza Strip, on the other hand, is much clearer: he asserts that the fall of Hamas is only a matter of months, and that it is, in any case, a non-negotiable prerequisite for the implementation of any peace agreement with the Palestinians.

On 17 February, Kosovo's unilateral declaration of independence provoked some reactions on the Palestinian side. Here is a territory which, thanks to the unfailing support of certain Western powers, has just succeeded in gaining independence. Serbia has been presented with a fait accompli. Some Palestinians see this as the new way forward.

On 26 February, in an interview with Voice of Palestine radio, Yasser Abed Rabbo[44] invited the Palestinian Authority to consider new options, arguing that its only strategy, 'negotiations at all costs,' was political suicide. Earlier, he had announced that the Palestinians would have to declare independence unilaterally if negotiations with Israel did not become more serious. The other PLO leaders, led by Abbas and Abu Alaa, immediately disavowed the dissident. The latter, hitherto close to the circle of negotiators, was pushed aside.

It's only through my housekeeper's little meals that bring me closer to the country. Palestinian specialties are close to her heart. Nahla is an odd character, though, with

----

44. A long-standing member of the Democratic Front for the Liberation of Palestine (DFLP), Yasser Abed Rabbo is best known for the Geneva Initiative, an unofficial Israeli–Palestinian peace plan made public in 2003. Close to Abbas, he is a member of the PLO executive committee.

a great strength of character. Occasionally, we have a little chat. To meet the needs of her five children and hospitalized husband, she toils tirelessly. She's intrigued by my single status. At my age, she finds it hard to understand why I'm not married yet. I have French nationality and earn a good living. She thinks it's heresy that I'm still single. She probably wonders why I've come to waste my time here, tilting at windmills, cranes, and Israeli diggers, when my family, my friends, my life, are in Paris.

*

I'm desperate to take my mind off things. With increasing frequency, I go to East Jerusalem in the evenings. Not that the city, which is slowly dying, is particularly attractive, but I'm trying to get out of the little bubble of Ramallah. But it's hard to break away from work. It's impossible to ignore the occupation. The road from Ramallah to Jerusalem always takes me back to it.

Forget the *checkpoints for a moment*—they're less crowded in the evening. As I approach the eastern part of the Holy City, I am assaulted by the inexorable advance of colonization.[45] It's impossible to ignore the construction work on the famous light rail line, which has left Bernard Kouchner, his predecessors and colleagues, speechless. It's all we can see: the construction work, being carried out by force in the Palestinian territories. Every day, they justify the confiscation of more land and the destruction of more homes.

---

45. See map p. 94.

'Palestitanic'

Recently, I've been passing the rail line under construction several times a week, as I dine in the vicinity of the *American Colony*, East Jerusalem's famous hotel. When Veolia[46] and Alstom won the Israeli government's 2005 tender for work in the Palestinian territories, nobody was fooled. The Quai d'Orsay had made sure that the responsibility of the French state could not be called into question because of future violations of international law engendered by this work in illegally occupied territories. It turns out that, legally speaking, the State of the fatherland of human rights risks nothing. The French ambassador was therefore able to attend the official ceremony celebrating the signing of the contract on 17 July 2005.

The companies undertook the work. Since then, whenever the PLO has questioned the Élysée or the Quai on this issue, the response has been the same: the government cannot be held responsible for the work carried out by French companies.[47] The result: Israeli construction is gradually shrinking Palestinian territory, thanks to the expertise of our companies.

No one seems able to stop the work. But day and night, the site is unguarded. In the evening, it's deserted, devoid of any human presence. Wouldn't blowing up the site be justified? A little dynamite would do the trick. The idea barely crosses my mind, and already, overcome by an uncontrollable guilt, I'm trying to brush it aside. And yet, given the

---

46. and various boycott threats, finally announced its withdrawal from the project in June 2009.

47. On the ambiguities of the French diplomatic position on this issue, see: http://blog.mondediplo.net/2007-10-24-Tramway-a-Jerusalem-mensonge-a-Paris

stakes involved and the general passivity, it wouldn't be so insane.

Desperate to banish these disturbing thoughts, I set off again for Ramallah. My mind continues to wander, bogged down in the throes of Israeli colonization and my participation in this damned negotiation process. I forget my way. The night is dark, and I quickly lose all hope of finding a sign pointing in the direction of Ramallah. I arrive in what looks like a settlement—Pisgat Zeev or Maale Adumim,[48] I imagine. The town is dead, each house identical to its neighbour. I drive in circles. Once, twice, three times: I can't find my way out of this parallel world, this piece of Israel in Palestine. At last, I come across a few suspicious shadows. Bearded, they seem to be wearing hats. Orthodox Jews, it seems. I could ask them for directions. But do they even know what Ramallah is? The Palestinian city seems lightyears away from this ominous place. I don't dare stop.

I decide to take a side road. I drive a few hundred metres, idling, until I finally come upon a familiar building: the wall. I breathe a *sigh of* relief—I must be near a *checkpoint*. I proceed along the wall, in a Pavlovian reflex, hoping to identify an entrance that would lead into the other world, that of the Palestinians. I see lights flickering in the distance. Two of them. Car lights? I approach at a slow pace. A vehicle is flashing its headlights at me. Suddenly, a much more powerful headlight comes on. Dazzled, I stop. A soldier has jumped out of the jeep. He points a gun at me and shouts in

---

48. See map p. 94.

'Palestitanic'

East Jerusalem
and surrounding areas

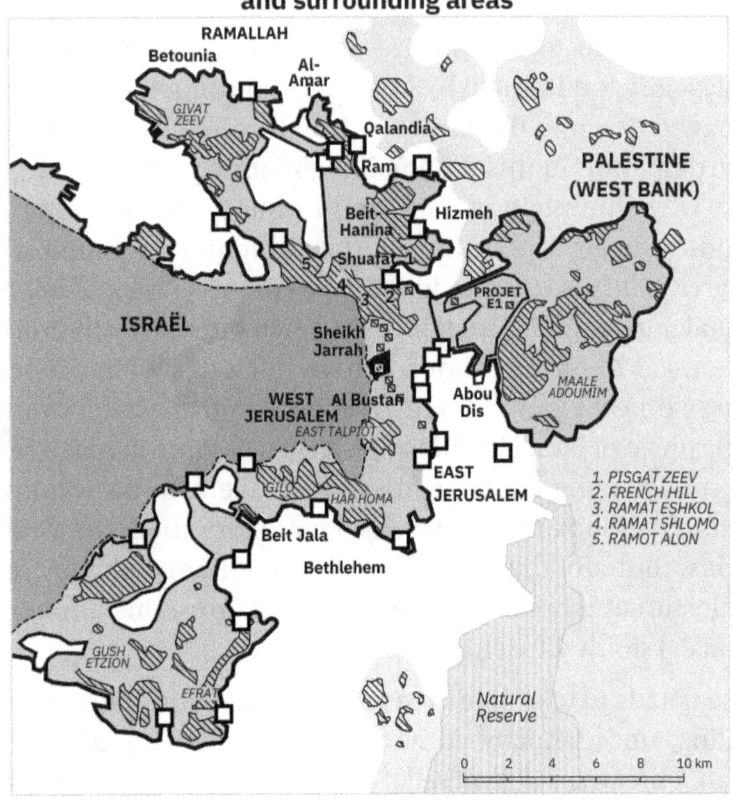

- – – –   Armistice line of 1949 ("green line")

▬   Old City of Jerusalem

▨   Settlements and outposts

SEPARATION WALL (IN OCTOBER 2009)

▬   Wall sections completed or in progress

▢   Main checkpoints

The E1 Project is an extention of the Maale Adumim Israeli settlement (industrial zones, hotels, city centers, dwellings).

▢   Palestinian municipal territories

▨   Territories on the Israeli side of the wall and *de facto* annexed territories

▢   Other territories controlled by settlements or the Israeli army

Settlement Access Routes

▨   Natural Reserve
Alternate North–South route
Palestinian transit (Wadi Nar)

Source: UN Office for the Coordination of Humanitarian Affairs (OCHA), Jerusalem, October 2009.

Hebrew. I throw myself out of the car, showing my passport. I shout too, in French. He continues to bellow, apparently even less reassured than I am. I try to calm him down and, continuing to wave my passport frantically, I explain, this time in English, that I'm lost. He gestures with his rifle: *Go, go!* He orders me to turn around, which I do in hurry. I'm already in the car, driving in the opposite direction, my hands clenched on the steering wheel. I drive straight ahead, staring into the night, not looking back. After a few kilometres, I find myself in familiar territory: a *checkpoint.* I'm relieved. Home is close.

*

I'm giving myself a little rest—no need to live dangerously. I've got a lot of work to do anyway. I might as well stay at home, close to the heating, as my Ramallahites neighbours do. While Nahla goes about her housework, I read the documents I haven't had time to study all week: Ehud Olmert has officially announced that negotiations on the borders have begun. At the same time, the destruction of Palestinian homes has redoubled. On 18 February, at another small committee meeting, Tzipi Livni explained to the Palestinians why she could not accept the 1967 borders. She wants an agreement that can be implemented. In other words, for her, the location of Jewish settlements in the West Bank will largely dictate the borders. Abu Alaa retorted that the 1967 borders must form the basis for territorial negotiations, even if certain adjustments to this line could be discussed.

Israel's wall on one side, human rights on the other; facts on the ground on one side, international law on the other It's a dialogue between the deaf.

At the meeting, Livni railed against the PLO: 'You can go on saying that you hate the settlement blocs and that they are a crime against humanity and contradict international legitimacy. Ultimately, it's up to you.'

The various negotiating committees have been formed. They cover the territories, bilateral relations, infrastructure, the economy, the culture of peace, prisoners, the environment, water, security, and legal issues. Jerusalem and refugees, the most sensitive issues, will be dealt with separately.

My name appears alongside those of Abu Alaa and Saeb Erekat in the 'refugees' box. Neither of them is an expert on the subject. Worse still, they show no particular interest in the plight of the refugees who make up 70 per cent of the Palestinian population.

I learn that the post of refugee negotiator has been offered to a number of figures whose competence on the issue is recognized: Nabil Shaath, Akram Haniyeh, Salim Tamari. One by one, they all declined. It's not hard to understand why: anyone who follows this conflict closely knows that if there is ever to be a two-state agreement, the PLO will have to give in on the refugee issue. On the PLO side, the right of return seems to have become opened to compromise, even though it is a right that every Palestinian has as an individual: the right to choose whether to return home or start a new life elsewhere. Those likely to negotiate the issue know this. While the right to return remains at the heart of the Palestinian identity, no one wants to take the blame. No one wants to become the traitor who sold out the rights of Palestinian refugees.

Nahla interrupts me to offer me a coffee. She stood in front of me. I looked up at her. She looks doubtful.

'Ziyad, can I ask you a question? she asks me.

'Of course, what is it?'

'There you go Ziyad, I really don't understand why you're still not married.'

I look at her, amused. I mime a sigh, before answering her:

'Listen, you know, morals are different in Europe. People often study for a long time before getting married. And sometimes, even, people live together, have children, without getting married. For me, it's also a matter of circumstance. Besides, I'm only thirty, which isn't that old!'

I smile at her, a little foolishly, in an attempt to punctuate my words. She stares at me in silence. She doesn't really look convinced. She concludes the conversation:

'Inshallah, you'll find a pretty Palestinian girl to marry here.'

'Inshallah,' I reply, before returning to my work.

I've barely had time to dive back into my reading when Nahla reappears. My housekeeper has removed her veil. She approaches me. I'm seated, at the mercy of her small, five-foot-five frame, wrinkled face, and downy moustache hair. Before I know what's happening, she puts her hand on my shoulder. She brings her lips close.

'Give me a kiss,' she says. Totally caught off guard, I place my hand between her face and mine:

'Nahla, no, that's wrong. How can you? You're married!'

She takes a step back but doesn't back down. She insists:

'Don't worry. My husband won't know. This will stay between you and me.'

I glare at her. Nahla takes refuge in the kitchen. A few moments later, I'm rescued by a friend who's come to take me for a walk into town. Nahla leaves the house, without a word, without farewell, along the wall. She has put her veil back on.

I hasten to tell Jacques, the friend in question, about my misadventure. My story amuses him to no end. I think aloud, half-seriously, 'You see, even at home, I'm not safe!'

*

Things are not getting any better in Gaza, far from it. News agency dispatches are tumbling across my computer screen, and with them, the ever-increasing death toll. On 27 February, the Israeli air force killed five Hamas militants. A new cycle of violence began. The Islamists responded with the traditional Qassam fire on Sderot and Katyusha fire on Ashkelon.[49] The Israelis retaliated, more massively. Incursions into Palestinian territory multiplied.

---

49. To visualize the location of Sderot and Ashkelon, see the "Israeltine" map, p. 225.

According to Palestinian sources, between 27 February and 3 March, the violence claimed 116 Palestinian victims, half of them civilians, including 22 children and 12 women. On the Israeli side, one civilian was killed when a rocket exploded at a university college near Sderot. Two Israeli soldiers were also killed during operations in Palestinian territory.

On 3 March, the Israeli army withdrew from the north of the territory without having succeeded in stopping the Palestinian missile fire. There's no doubt that these incursions will resume at some point, since the strategists at the Israeli Ministry of Defence have come up with nothing better to settle Gaza's fate.

Two days earlier, we were informed by the PLO's negotiations department that talks with the Israelis were once again suspended—nonsense. The peace process is a spectacle, a farce, played out at the expense of Palestinian reconciliation, at the cost of bloodshed in Gaza. And in spite of myself, I'm becoming one of the players, albeit a minor one, in this drama. I had been warned, of course; I had my own doubts. But never, never would I have imagined that in such a short space of time I would be convinced that we were heading for disaster. It's only the beginning of March, and I'm already wondering what I'm doing here. Perhaps it would be wiser to resign, to leave this ship which is certain to sink: the 'Palestitanic,' as some of my friends and family affectionately call her.

Despite the tragedy in Gaza, despite the explosion of settlements, despite the complete lack of good faith on the part of the Israelis in the peace talks, the PLO will continue to negotiate, against all odds. A headlong rush to negotiate. Because the PLO has decided it has no other choice. Because the political survival of its old guard is at stake, of course. Because, after decades of struggle, Arafat's last companions, those still supported at arm's length by the 'international community,' believe that the creation of the Palestinian state is not so far off. Unless, after three Arab–Israeli wars and two Intifadas, the Palestinians simply can't take it anymore. Who could blame them?

Military incursions have also resumed here in Ramallah. The other evening, I passed three Israeli jeeps a few steps from my house. I was coming back from a happy dinner with friends. Israeli soldiers were cleaning up in a nearby refugee camp. I heard gunshots. They became frequent, but only at night. I go to bed early. I try to ignore it all.

*

The publication of an investigation by the American magazine *Vanity Fair* entitled 'The Gaza Bombshell'[50] is the last straw for me. It's at the office that I read this skilfully detailed article, which shows in a new light two years of turmoil leading up to the Hamas coup in Gaza. Here are the main points:

Following Hamas's victory in the legislative elections of January 25, 2006, Mahmoud Abbas initially tried to facilitate the establishment of a government of national unity. But Washington was not on the same wavelength. On

---

50. ROSE (David), "The Gaza Bombshell", *Vanity Fair*, April 2008.

October 4, 2006, Condoleezza Rice went to Ramallah to meet the Palestinian president. She explained that trying to isolate Hamas was not enough: Abu Mazen must dissolve the government of new Prime Minister Ismail Haniyeh as soon as possible and organize new elections. The President of the Palestinian Authority, a staunch American ally, agreed. He will comply a month later.

Everyone knows that this about-turn will provoke violent reactions from Hamas. The United States therefore decided to provide Abu Mazen with solid guarantees. Fatah would receive material and political support, and its security forces would be reinforced. The Bush administration also insisted that Abu Mazen's team include authority figures. Mohammad Dahlan, the former head of preventive security in Gaza, the man of dirty work, is back.

At the end of 2006, the American program began to take shape. Rice stepped up contacts with Egypt, Jordan, Saudi Arabia and the United Arab Emirates, urging them to contribute to the financing, training and development of Fatah forces. At the end of December 2006, four Egyptian trucks arrived in Gaza via an Israeli crossing. Their contents were received by Fatah. The delivery was leaked to the media. A member of the Israeli cabinet declares on the radio that the rifles and ammunition will give Abbas 'the ability to stand up to the organizations that are trying to sabotage everything'. Hamas is directly targeted.

On February 1, 2007, Dahlan's forces stormed the Islamic University of Gaza. Hamas responded with attacks on Fatah police stations. For fear of being held responsible for triggering a civil war, Mahmoud Abbas suddenly backed down.

For weeks, King Abdullah of Saudi Arabia had been trying to persuade him to meet Hamas in Mecca, so that a government of national unity could be formed. Abbas finally went on February 6, accompanied by Dahlan. Although Hamas still refused to recognize Israel, an agreement was reached. At the same time, the Saudis promised to pay the salaries of the Palestinian Authority, which had been frozen by the international community since Hamas won the elections. Fatah and Hamas supporters celebrate the news together in Gaza.

The United States decided to respond by redoubling the pressure on its Palestinian allies. They were determined to put an end to the coalition government and devised a 'Plan B'. The aim is to force the establishment of a Palestinian government that accepts the Quartet's principles. If Hamas refuses to revise its position towards Israel, Abbas will have to precipitate the fall of the government.

This plan gave rise to a document entitled 'Action Plan for the Palestinian Presidency'. Drawn up by the Americans, it was submitted to the PLO and the Jordanians for comment. Early versions of the plan emphasized the need to support Fatah forces in order to counter Hamas' designs. They detail measures to reinforce its security personnel, including the provision of 4,700 additional men, dispatched in new battalions trained in Egypt and Jordan. Abbas must be put in a position to take any emergency decisions that may be required.

The ultimate objective of the Action Plan is formulated as follows: 'To enable the establishment of the security that will be able to protect and strengthen a peaceful

There Will Be No Palestinian State

Palestinian state living side by side with Israel.' Its latest version is being finalized in Ramallah by Palestinian Authority officials. It is identical to the documents discussed earlier. With one exception: the Plan is now presented as a Palestinian initiative.

On April 30, 2007, an extract from the Plan was published in the Jordanian press. For Hamas, the message was clear: Fatah was preparing a coup d'état with the support of the United States. While the formation of a government of national unity had restored calm in the territories, these revelations led to renewed violence.

Unfortunately for Fatah, the Palestinian Authority forces in Gaza have to do without their leader: Dahlan has just undergone knee surgery. Convalescing in Berlin, he will be out of action for several weeks.

In mid-May, while Dahlan was still away, 500 new recruits from the Palestinian national security forces arrived in Gaza. Freshly trained in Egypt, they were equipped with new weapons and brand-new vehicles. Their arrival was immediately noticed. These new troops are instantly attacked by Hamas. By the end of May 2007, Hamas attacks had become a regular occurrence, with unprecedented violence.

On June 7, the *Haaretz* newspaper reported that Mahmoud Abbas and the Americans had asked Israel to authorize a new arms shipment from Egypt. This was to include dozens of armoured cars, hundreds of rockets, thousands of grenades and millions of rounds of ammunition. A few days later, Hamas decided to take matters seriously.

'Palestitanic'

On June 15, 2007, following bloody clashes in which 113 people were killed, Fatah security forces were dislodged from the Gaza Strip. Hamas, the 'Islamic Resistance Movement,' took control of the Palestinian territory, to the disgust of Fatah, the United States, Israel and their Arab and Western allies.

*

I finish reading the article. I'm floored. I stand still for long minutes, as if catatonic. Finally, I manage to get up. Desperate for a sensible move, I open my office window. The red sun is setting over Ramallah. The city of La Sulta is bustling and noisy, as it always is at the end of the day. The facts reported by the survey confirm my initial reservations and the impressions nourished by my first weeks here. I'm caught in a vice: what do I think of the Annapolis process now?

It takes me a few minutes to put all the pieces together. Mahmoud Abbas was persuaded by his American ally in the hope of returning to the negotiating table with Israel, so he agreed to cooperate in liquidating Hamas. Against the unity of his people, Abu Mazen rallied to George W. Bush's plan.

It's now much clearer; I've just grasped the full cruelty of the environment in which my role as advisor to the PLO takes place. I'm distraught. I write an e-mail to the NSU manager expressing my deepest reservations about continuing my mission in the light of the existence of the infamous American 'action plan.' After much rereading, I sent my message, like throwing a bottle into the sea. My missive, my call for help, went unanswered.

*

I try to relax, as best I can. I'm taking it easy. My good Palestinian resolutions have come to nothing. I now buy whatever I feel like at the supermarket, including the occasional Israeli product. I haven't used the Qalandia *checkpoint* for a few days now. Fear of breaking down, no doubt. To get to Jerusalem, I now use the Hizme checkpoint,[51] which is mainly used by Israeli settlers. I'm rarely checked there. Clean-shaven and dressed in a suit, driving my car with Israeli plates, I look like a settler. It's all a question of attitude: with the window half-open and the car radio tuned to Israeli techno, I don't glance in the direction of the soldiers. I barely slow down: I'm a settler, I tell you! The military can do their job. They're not here for me.

More rarely, I use the Beit El 'VIP' *checkpoint*, open to diplomats, accredited organizations, and important individuals. There are no queues. The soldiers are polite, even smiling sometimes. From time to time, I get a 'good day.' Beit El is occupation with a human face, only for a privileged few, mainly foreigners. For me, who wagered foolishly on the prospect of peace with the Israelis. For me, who, thanks to Adam Smith International, enjoys a 'free pass.'

---

51. See map p. 94.

I exercise to try and clear my head, to try and forget these ambient doldrums. For the past few weeks, I've been feverish every time I turn the ignition on my car. A dreadful apprehension, albeit slight, but recurrent. I don't feel safe. I have a feeling of being watched, of having enemies. Flashes of the political assassinations perpetrated by Mossad against members of the PLO in the 70s and 80s come to mind. Images of the bloody reprisals between Hamas sympathizers and Fatah supporters obsess me. It's irrepressible.

I came to Palestine to make myself useful—I didn't want to take sides in this internal Palestinian split. However, because of my responsibilities, I chose a side. Despite all the precautions I took, I erred on the side of naivety. Perhaps also out of vanity, since the outfit of the peace-keeper is so flattering to wear. I chose negotiation rather than continuing the fight against the occupier. In my defence, I was better trained to follow the first path. It's also a less costly choice. Would I have risked my life for Palestine? Would I have endangered my life in its defence? I'm desolate. Everything suggests that the choice of negotiation will be futile. Worse, everything suggests that it will be paid for dearly.

I now understand that the Palestinian Authority, over the years, has become an occupying force. It has been reduced to doing the dirty work in the West Bank in place of the Israelis, with the support of the Americans and the European Union. Having considered every angle, and given the stakes involved, I refuse to leave my position at the NSU prematurely. At this stage, the refugees undoubtedly need an advocate from within. At least I'm in a good position to know what's going on in the negotiations.

Nevertheless, my decision risks making me just another puppet in the hands of the Israelis, one of many inconsistent acts, waving in the middle of the peace circus. I'm under their control, at their mercy. Perhaps I've also become a target for Hamas. As we emerge from winter, as the weather softens, I'm anxious.

*

Today, 10 March 2008, I went swimming. As is often the case, I spent the weekend working. Nevertheless, I managed to give myself half a day's rest. I returned home after a soothing effort and, after a good dinner, went to bed. A few twinges of nerves upset me as I got out of the pool, and then again during my meal. Nothing too serious, just a tingling sensation.

Once in bed, the pain suddenly becomes unbearable. Like stabbing blades, they tear at my heart. I'm soon immobilized, almost unable to breathe. I'm suffocating. Before long, my shoulder and arm are paralyzed. I try to relax, 'This will pass,' I tell myself. It won't. I reach for my mobile to call for help. It's no use. I try to turn around to find a less uncomfortable position. Another failure. Long minutes go by without the pain subsiding. My breathing, hindered by the pain, is panting. I suck in air from the corner of my mouth. I'm not going to last long like this, that's for sure. There's no doubt about it: my time has come.

My grandfather died of a heart attack. At a young age. Like him, one of my uncles suddenly died of heart failure. He was not yet thirty. Heart attacks are said to be a Palestinian disease.[52]

Time passes, and I'm still alive. My agony continues, even though night has been falling for a long time now. Failing to master the pain, I try to regain a little serenity. I start reciting my prayers, without conviction, to calm myself. But over time, I've forgotten my professions of faith. My 'Our Father' is rusty. My 'Hail Mary' is numb. Fortunately, 'Fatiha' recently came to mind thanks to the intervention of an Israeli envoy. Sometimes angels don't appear at best days. Remember, it was in Jerusalem, *Al Quds* or *Yerushalem*[53] as you like. I cursed him at the time. I was mistaken. May God bless his soul. May God forgive me. I start reciting the Fatiha over and over, without restraint. As my existence teeters on the brink, I cling to the only scrap of revealed word I can remember. I recite it, I repeat the Fatiha, over and over again, like a Sufi, in the hope that my spirit will finally give way. I get drunk on words I barely understand as I pray for appeasement.

At last, the call to prayer rings out. It heralds the coming dawn. Genetics has not condemned me—Palestinian fate has not taken me. My delirium has come to an end. I haven't slept all night, but I'm still here. I'm still alive. My bruised flesh is my witness. The pain remains violent.

---

52. A doctor once told me that the population of the territories had the highest rate of heart attacks in the world. I didn't check.
53. *Al Quds* means Jerusalem in Arabic; *Yerushalem*, in Hebrew.

I decide to wait until eight o'clock. At eight o'clock, I'll call for help. After nearly ten hours of agony, which felt like a hundred, it was my friend Karim who I called. We're off to Hadassah hospital in Jerusalem. Thank God my French passport allows me to avoid treatment in the occupied Palestinian territories.

*

I've missed three days of work by the time I'm back at the office, despite the stabbing pain. My work colleagues are worried. But they don't seem surprised.

The inconclusive medical diagnosis suggests that the pain was caused by a pulled intercostal muscle. The NSU thinks otherwise: everyone's convinced I had a panic attack. Everyone has had a similar experience of their own. One tells me he's been there too, not so long ago. Another says he's still under the care of a psychotherapist. Some of my colleagues manage their stress, even their despair, with a pronounced taste for alcohol. I'm not there yet.

Anyway, I don't have time to feel sorry for myself. 'Officially,' negotiations between Israel and the PLO resumed on 5 March. *The show must go on.* Meetings have been held in committees, only on issues that the Israelis are willing to discuss. At the highest political level, the focus is still on borders and security issues, with no progress being made. The Israelis remain fixated on their separation wall that's firmly in place. Jerusalem, rejected in its entirety to the west of the wall in Israel, has no reason to be discussed.

On this issue, it's always the army of the Jewish state, with its shovels and cranes, who do the work instead of the negotiators. As far as the refugees are concerned, I've had confirmation that Saeb Erekat has indeed received the file from Tal Becker, his Israeli counterpart.

I was also asked to sit on a committee dealing with 'the culture of peace.' I must confess that I didn't take the proposal seriously. Perhaps mistakenly, I thought that before talking about a culture of peace, Israel had to be able to treat its interlocutor as an equal and agree to negotiate in good faith the issues that were really in conflict. I declined the offer.

The circus tent now seems to be firmly in place. The NSU is worried that the PLO has no plan B if the peace talks fail. Mahmoud Abbas has told his advisors that if no agreement is reached before the end of the year, he will resign as President of the Palestinian Authority—that's a relief.

On 27 March, George W. Bush informed him that he would soon be invited to Washington. The official objective announced by the White House spokesman is to relaunch talks between Israelis and Palestinians.

But what other fresh hell awaits?

VII
HAIFA
APRIL 2008

I'm relieved to see the first days of spring arrive and, with them, Benoît, a friend from Paris. Without delay, we decide to leave for a few days. On our way to the north of the country, we stop in Haifa.[54]

Anyone familiar with Beirut will find here the Levantine flavour of the neighbouring Lebanese capital. Both cities share the Mediterranean, even if Haifa's hills, Mount Carmel, also give it a false San Francisco air. I don't know if Haifa is beautiful. I'm in no position to say: my mother's family came from there. My grandfather, Habib Sanbar, was Honorary Consul of Lebanon in Palestine and administrator of this once-flourishing port.

I never knew my grandfather. My mother confessed to me that one day she saw her elder sister crying, and, copying her, she shed her own tears. Habib died in 1951 or 1952, I don't know. He left behind a widow and six children.

After the Nakba, the head of the family went into exile in Arabia. The prosperous Levantine consul had become

---

54. See maps p. 8.

merely an accountant in the desert. With the creation of Israel, he had lost all his personal property, confiscated by the new state. The property and wealth he managed for the neighbouring state he returned to the Lebanese government. He and his family were offered citizenship of Lebanon, the Land of Cedars. My grandfather, a patriot, refused the? Lebanese citizenship for himself. As a father, he however accepted the gift for his wife and children who became Lebanese nationals. His country had suddenly vanished. He became stateless. What remained was honour, the nobility of virtue and the love of his family. Emigrating to the Gulf, Habib continued to write poems to his wife, my grandmother, who had taken refuge with the rest of the family in Lebanon. She never remarried. Habib's heart stopped beating the day he was told that a Hebrew university had been built on his land in Palestine—that's what I was told.

That's all I know—my mother was too young to remember anything more. Out of privacy, for fear of lifting the veil over which the family has rebuilt itself, I never questioned the other siblings. I reappropriated what I had been given. In my mind, my grandfather died with Palestine, for Palestine, because of Palestine.

The day before I left Paris, my mother gave me a copy of our property deeds. Our land, 'absentee property' under Israeli law, has been confiscated for nearly sixty years. God knows what I'm going to do with these papers. For the moment, it's not a question of following in my grandfather's footsteps. I'm not ready, not willing, to discover the family home that seems to have survived the passage of time and the upheavals of this tumultuous region, to take possession of this past that still eludes me, that remains for me always foreign, in fact. I've never quite known how to take it all in. The time will come, naturally. Today, it's still too early. In any case, we've decided to stop here only briefly, on our way to Acre, a few kilometres to the north.

Ever since we arrived in Haifa, I've had a lump in my throat. I'm trying to hide my confusion. Benoît and I have sat down to lunch on one of the terraces along the pleasant avenue around which the lower town of Haifa is organized. This airy thoroughfare is called Ben-Gurion Avenue. It links the port to the Baha'i Palace and its tiered, flower-filled gardens. The perspective is magnificent. The population here is mixed: a few tourists, Arabs and a few Jews, mainly Russian speaking. The occupation of the West Bank is far off, and the oppressive situation in Jerusalem forgotten. The feeling that prevails here also contrasts with the somewhat superficial detachment that reigns in Tel Aviv. This place is obviously steeped in history, but the Mediterranean, and that gentle breeze from the port, soften its heaviness.

I open a guidebook by two American Palestinian journalists. Entitled *Palestine,* the book devotes a long chapter to Haifa, Israel. I skim the dozen or so pages on the city from which my grandfather was torn. The Mediterranean city dates back at least two millennia. It has always been rich and cosmopolitan. At the turn of the 20th century, it was the creation of the Haifa-Damascus-La Mecca railroad line that triggered an explosion of economic development. In 1929, the Kirkuk-Haifa *pipeline* was inaugurated, and, thanks to the Palestinian port, Iraqi oil found an outlet to the Mediterranean and the rest of the world. Haifa had become the second-largest Mediterranean port, just behind Marseille. With the influx of workers and the development of trade, immigrants, intellectuals, trade unions, and newspapers began to flourish. So did Jewish immigration. Having visited the region at the end of the previous century, Theodore Herzl had also succumbed to Haifa's charms.

At the end of the Second World War, Haifa's Arabs lived alongside Armenians, Greeks, Persians, Indians, Jews, Germans, and other Arabs, most of them Lebanese. Following the UN partition of Palestine on 29 November 1947, Haifa became part of the Jewish state, despite the opposition of the vast majority of its population. The day after the partition, the Irgun[55] and the Haganah[56] created a climate of terror in the city, multiplying attacks on Arab neighbourhoods. A wave of panic swept through the population, leading to a first wave of emigration. The campaign of aggression and intimidation intensified until April 1948. It culminated on 21 April when the Carmel Brigade, one of

---

55. The Irgun is a Zionist armed organization founded in 1931 in Mandatory Palestine, following a split with the Haganah. It was responsible for numerous terrorist attacks against the Arab population of Palestine. After the creation of Israel, most Irgun elements were integrated into the regular army.
56. The Haganah, which means 'defence' in Hebrew, was a clandestine Zionist organization founded in 1920 as a protection force for Jewish émigrés in Palestine. The organization later became the unofficial military arm of the Jewish Agency, the Zionist executive in Palestine, whose aim was to promote the establishment of a Jewish state. When Israel was founded in 1948, the Haganah joined forces with the Irgun and another militia, the Stern Group, to form Tsahal, the Israeli Defense Force.

the Jewish army's elite units, went on the offensive, driving Haifa's Arabs into flight.

Out of a population of 61,000, only 3,500 Arabs were able to remain in Haifa. The fleeing Arab population found refuge in Lebanon. Those who were expelled or fled the fighting were never able to return. Most Palestinian homes were confiscated by the Israeli state and have since been rented out to Jewish families. Today, the majority of Haifa's Arab residents come from the Palestinian villages around the port city and in the Galilee that were destroyed. They account for around 10 per cent of the city's 300,000 inhabitants. Despite this painful past, Haifa is often seen today as a model of cohabitation between Jews and Arabs. The port city, though a little decayed, remains welcoming.

I look up from my book. I've forgotten about Benoît and the terrace where we're sitting. My surroundings are a little surreal. The restaurant's customers compete in accents, but all seem to share the satisfaction of exposure to the first rays of sunshine of the year. Jews or Arabs, they all smoke hookahs. Our restaurant even plays a few classics by Fairuz, the voice of Lebanon. The diva could be singing from across the border, and you'd almost hear her. The Lebanese 'enemy' is only a few dozen kilometres away.

Lunch wolfed down, it's time for us to get back on the road to Acre. Benoît pretends to glance at the map. He folds up the map. With an air of determination, he calls out to me:

'Are we going to see your grandfather's house?'

His question paralyzes me.

'It's now or never, isn't it? Apparently, we're right next door...'

I take the map of Haifa from his hands. The Wadi Nisnas neighbourhood, where the family home is located, is indeed nearby.

I look at him, silent and thoughtful. I finally open my mouth:

'I'm not ready. It's not the right time. I'll go later.'

He insists, 'Come on, this is ridiculous. If we don't go, you'll regret it.'

'No, no, I don't feel like it. Not today.'

Benoît doesn't care about my reservations. He gets up and sets off. After a moment's hesitation, I follow him.

*

We walk in the direction of Wadi Nisnas. With no further indication of the exact location of the house, I reassure myself that it's unlikely we'll find it anyway. The excursion wasn't on the agenda, so I hadn't thought it useful to be told the exact location of the family home by my mother.

After a ten-minute walk, we arrive at Wadi Nisnas. The neighbourhood is just a stone's throw from Ben-Gurion Avenue. I fall in love with it instantly. It's Saturday. Shabbat is market day here, and fruit and vegetable vendors bustle about under the benevolent flag of the Israeli Communist Party, which sits in the centre of this predominantly Arab community. The produce stalls are a delight to the senses: apples, pears, watermelons, apricots, strawberries, eggplants, medlars, oranges, lemons... I'm amazed. Everything is fresh and appetizing. The scent of fruit mingles with the stronger smells of the fishmongers and the gentle breeze from the nearby harbour below. Idioms jostle happily: Arabic and Hebrew collide with a few Russian accents. I pass Asian faces in the narrow streets. Where do these people come from? Ports, places of passage par excellence, are always full of surprises.

I'm happy to be here. Benoît also seems to be enjoying the place. The neighbourhood's main street, now called Yohanan Haqadosh, is a narrow shopping street that winds downhill towards the port. I notice the casual attire of the people milling about on what is normally a non-working day in Israel: in this spring sunshine, shorts are de rigueur. They're worn as much by young, boisterous Arab teenagers as they are by elderly Ashkenazi Jews with ruddy complexions. No veils in sight. It's a far cry from the Orthodox Jewish quarter of Mea Sharim in Jerusalem, or even Ramallah, where most women now go out with their heads covered.

I finally decide to ask for directions and try to locate the family home. I spot two old gentlemen sitting on a chair, drinking tea. Incidentally, I ask them if they know where *Beit Sanbar*, the Sanbars' home, is. I explain that my grandfather, Habib Sanbar, a '1948 refugee' as we say here, is from Wadi Nisnas. As luck would have it, my interlocutors seem to have a good memory of the area. They explain that I need to go down the street and that I'll find two houses further down: the first belongs to the Sanbars who still live in Haifa, the second to the 'Lebanese Sanbars,' as he calls them, who were forced to flee at the time of the Nakba. I deduce that my grandfather's house is the second.

I walk down the street with Benoît. It's much less lively as we walk towards the port. We pass an Episcopal church. We pass a little lady carrying shopping bags. Once again, I ask for directions:

'Do you know where the Sanbar house is?'

The woman raises her eyes to mine, as if to stare at me. She smiles at me, with an air of connivance.

'Of course I know where the Sanbar house is. That's where I live.'

Her answer takes my breath away. I try to pull myself together. I tell her I'm one of the grandchildren of Habib Sanbar, who lived here with his family until 1948.

Always friendly, never shy, this woman invites us to follow her. We pass the porch of the house. The house, now divided in two: she tells me that the first dwelling, recently renovated, is inhabited by her husband's cousins. She lives with her husband and children in a second, more run-down building, which faces a small garden. She invites us to sit down on her terrace and offers us a cup of tea.

Our hostess is of Egyptian–Lebanese origin. She is married to a Palestinian. She explains that her husband's family fled a nearby village, destroyed by Zionist forces in 1948. When the fighting ended, these Palestinians found refuge in this empty house. My grandfather's house. They've lived there ever since. Surprisingly, the situation is more uncomfortable for me than for her. I'm almost embarrassed to disturb her environment. She occupies a property that belongs to my grandfather, but she's showing a willingness to make my acquaintance. She asks about my family. At no time does she give me the impression that she perceives my friend and me as a threat.

We leave the house shortly afterwards. We bid farewell to our hostess, and I thanked her for her kindness. Benoît took a few photos of me in front of the porch. We walk up the street. I suggest we stop for coffee in a little boui-boui. The place is run by an old Palestinian woman. The menu is in Hebrew, but she serves traditional homemade Palestinian dishes: *faitoulia, moujadarra,* grape leaves... Emotion catches up with me. I get goose bumps. I can feel Haifa through every pore of my skin. Tears roll down my cheeks. Palestine, *my* Palestine, my mother's Palestine, didn't die the day my family fled. It survives here. Israel or not, life hasn't stopped.

I had a Turkish coffee, very strong. And very sweet, *ziyaada,* as we say here. Coffee grounds still on my tongue, the smell of cardamom in my nose, I'm now strolling through the streets of Wadi Nisnas. I'm no longer on a quest; I'm no longer looking for anything. I'm just wandering. I'm at ease. In Haifa, I'm at home.

*

Later, I'll tell my mother about my return to Haifa. She has no real memories of Palestine. But today, at last, I know what little she does know. It took me thirty years and a trip to the occupied territories for my mother to recount what she knows of the first months of her life.

My mother should never have been born. My grand-mother, already the mother of five children, had an accident while carrying her in her womb. Her doctor concluded that it would be safer for her health to have an abortion. Accompanied by her husband, she went to the Haifa hospital for the operation. A Jewish doctor was her provider that day. Everything was in place to terminate the pregnancy. It was a power outage that saved my mother—and the faith of the Jewish doctor and the faith of his Christian patients. All agreed that it was a sign of destiny. A few months later, my mother was born in perfect health.

My mother was born in Palestine on 6 October 1947. In troubled times, a month and a half before the partition of the country on 29 November. Little Jihan fled the country in her mother's arms when she was only a few weeks old, without her father, who initially decided to stay, in the hope of a return to calm. So, my grandfather put his wife and six children on a boat, bound for Beirut. The port of Haifa had already fallen under the control of Zionist forces. According to my mother, the Jewish militiamen let my family get on the boat because of the bassinet, her newborn child. It was a one-way trip.

*

More than sixty years later, the final terms of the Israeli–Palestinian schism remain unresolved. And with them, the fate of the Palestinian refugees' right of return. It's early April 2008, and negotiations are still at a standstill. One day, however, I am summoned for an initial meeting with

There Will Be No Palestinian State

Saeb Erekat. The Israelis would be willing to discuss the refugees. Dr Saeb wanted to meet with his experts to identify the points on which the parties needed to agree.

Accompanied by a colleague, I get a short meeting. The interview is rushed. Dr Saeb pays little attention. He is distracted. Visibly uncomfortable, he confesses that he does not wish to negotiate the case himself. If he does, even temporarily, it's only because Abu Alaa has asked him to. But he is frank enough to admit that he is not competent enough to discuss the refugee issue with the Israelis. Nevertheless, he tries to be reassuring; he still hopes to find the right person to take over from him. We nod in agreement, without conviction. Given the emotional charge attached to the problem, the totally asymmetrical balance of power between Israel and the PLO, and the prevailing scepticism about the Annapolis process, I doubt that Saeb Erekat will find a taker.

In the days that followed, I heard nothing from Dr Saeb. Did he discuss the refugees with Tal Becker, the Israeli negotiator? All I know is that a meeting was scheduled between them. It wasn't until a week later that the NSU coordinator finally came to see me in my office. She hands me a document:

'Here is the first written proposal from the Israelis. It was forwarded by Tal [Becker] to Saeb. Saeb wants us to prepare a response based on this offer.'

I read the document[57] It's half a page long. I return to my colleague. I smile ruefully:

---

57. The first document on refugees submitted by the Israeli delegation is reproduced in Appendix I.

'We're not going to answer that, is this a joke?'

'Yes, that's what Saeb asked.'

'But do you even know if he bothered to read the document? We can't reasonably start working on that basis...'

'I assume he's read it. I'm just reporting his instructions. If you have any problems with them, just give him a call and take it up with him.'

I do have a problem with the instructions. The Israeli document ignores almost all the rights recognized by law and the international community for Palestinian refugees.[58] Beyond the thorny question of the right to return, the document fails to mention fair compensation for the harm suffered. But it's hard for me to question the Palestinian *Chief Negotiator's* instructions. I've only just arrived—he doesn't know me. The train is moving, so we'll just have to grit our teeth and get on with it.

*

I call for a small internal meeting at the NSU to discuss how to proceed. I am of the mind that the PLO cannot agree to work on the basis of a document prepared by the Israelis, which deliberately misses the point. This would be

---

58. The rights of Palestinian refugees under international law can be summarized as follows: recognition of Israel's responsibility for creating and perpetuating the refugee problem; recognition and implementation of the right of return; restitution of Palestinian refugee property; when restitution of property is not materially possible, or when the refugee wishes his material losses to be made good *through* compensation, the corresponding financial compensation, as well as that relating to non-material damage suffered as a result of his long-term and forced exile. For further information, see, for example: http://www.badil.org/fr.

tantamount to capitulation, plain and simple, before the discussions had even begun. Refugees are *the* Palestinian issue. The Palestinians are a people of exiles; it is essential that the PLO regain control of this issue.

The discussion with my NSU colleagues quickly turns into trench warfare. As legal counsel, I'm told to stay in my lane. I'm reminded in hushed tones that I'm a newcomer and that I wasn't recruited to oppose the party line. I still don't have the confidence of my team and the NSU management, who are putting me under pressure.

Although in the minority, I don't give in. We finally reach a compromise: we would offer Saeb two options. In accordance with his instructions, the first will be to submit a document protecting our positions but taking up the structure of the article proposed by the Israelis. The second will be to submit a *'non-paper,'* a document that carries no legal commitment, which will enable us to start discussions with our interlocutor on a more solid basis: the law and the various interests involved. The aim is to steer Saeb Erekat towards the second path, while enabling him to make an informed choice.

We are summoned to Saeb's office in the negotiations department. It's crowded, and we're not given much time. Saeb juggles between checking his latest e-mails and the asides of his colleagues in the room. I finally manage to get his attention. I hand him the documents as I explain. I don't dwell on the first option; I take the time to clarify the advantages of the second. He looks at the two papers. Visually, the second document is much more appealing.[59]

---

59. The Palestinian *non-paper* on refugees is reproduced in Appendix II.

Saeb Erekat concludes our conference with an 'Okay, thank you.' He packs up and heads off to another meeting. I've made sure that the document we prefer is in the right place in his file.

I received confirmation two days later that Dr Saeb had indeed followed our advice. He presented the *non-paper,* provoking the ire of Tzipi Livni's chief of staff. According to Saeb, who looks pleased with himself, Tal Becker even threatened to leave the meeting room.

I have no illusions. We haven't regained control of the situation. But at least this first stumbling block has been overcome, without any apparent damage. I haven't betrayed anyone—not Eissam, the driver from the Chatila refugee camp; not Habib, the grandfather I never knew. The return to Haifa, my grandfather's house, my home, is still on the negotiating table.

*

As planned, Mahmoud Abbas and his advisors visited the White House. By his own admission, the visit was a failure. On 25 April, at the end of these meetings in Washington, the president of Sulta disclosed that there had been no progress in bilateral Israeli–Palestinian negotiations. Bush does not consider it appropriate to exert further pressure on Israel to allow a settlement freeze. Even on the American side, no one dares speak of the 1967 borders as the basis for the territorial demarcation between Israel and Palestine. The PLO leader leaves, satisfied with only one thing from the summit: the US administration heard his message that the Palestinians cannot accept anything other than a full and final peace agreement before the end of the year. The PLO will not accept yet another partial agreement or declaration of intent.

At his press conference the day before, Bush seemed to scale down his objective: by the end of 2008, a Palestinian state must be *defined. It is* no longer a question of *creating* this state, as had been asserted with great fanfare at Annapolis. Abbas's message may have been heard, but it will not be heeded. Quite the opposite—according to his entourage, the American president is delighted to be travelling to Israel in a few days' time to attend the celebrations surrounding the sixtieth anniversary of the only state in the Holy Land to date.

VIII
Nakba
May 2008

More and more flags bearing the Star of David fly all over Israel. Not only in Israel, but also in the occupied territories, where the colours of the Hebrew State, worn like a banner, float on the cars of settlers, in the faces of their Palestinian neighbours.

On 15 May, Israel will celebrate sixty years of existence, of oppression. For the Palestinians, 15 May 2008 marks the 60th commemoration of the Nakba. I bought my little Palestinian flag and hung it on my car too. But there's no option of showing this Palestinian patriotism in Israel, naturally. In the Palestinian territories? Between two Israeli checkpoints at most, at a respectful distance from the soldiers. The more than 200 *checkpoints* on the West Bank quickly break my proselytizing spirit. So I restrict my display to a handful of kilometres at most, to a piece of Zone A of these Bantustans[60] that people insist on calling Palestine.

---

60. Bantustans were regions created during the apartheid era in South Africa and South-West Africa. Reserved for the Black population, they enjoyed a certain degree of autonomy. In 1970, the Bantustans were renamed 'national homes' (called *tuislands* or *homelands*) by the South African author-

After just a few days, I decided to remove the little Palestinian flag. The poor-quality plastic attachment wouldn't fit my window anyway.

Israel hosts an array of events to celebrate, attended by numerous international delegations. The American President is scheduled to address the Knesset[61] To express his dissatisfaction with the continuation of Israel's fait accompli amidst the peace process, Mahmoud Abbas already announced that foreign diplomats attending the festivities will not be welcome in Ramallah. I'm not sure his intention will be understood.

For my part, I checked the date of 15 May as soon as I arrived here. In this year of negotiations, the voice of refugees must be heard on the international stage. The Nakba commemoration is the perfect time to make our voices heard. I am viscerally convinced that peace is inconceivable without due consideration of Palestinian history and identity. However, I cannot deny the obvious: the PLO is not positioned to obtain these outcomes alone from the Israelis at the negotiating table. Our only chance is in the court of public opinion. I've already told Saeb that I'm planning a number of communication operations to this end: journalist visits to the camps, briefings, a press release on the situation and rights of the refugees, and a column by President Abbas in the international press.

---

ities. By extension, the word *Bantustan* now designates any territory whose inhabitants are discriminated against and treated as second-class citizens within their own country.
61. The Knesset is the Israeli parliament.

*

I soon realize that things may not go my way. The NSU's communications department doesn't share my enthusiasm for the approaching deadline. They've seen it all before, and the return of the refugees is not immediate. To make matters worse, we're without Xavier, one of our most motivated people.

This young Chilean Palestinian associate[62] is, above all, an activist and a patriot. An eminently likeable character, Xavier is easy to get along with. He rarely separates from his keffiyeh, worn over his shoulders, and his gold cross, displayed with aplomb. His family hails from Beit Jala,[63] a stone's throw from Bethlehem. He decided to settle there, despite the settlements that are nibbling away at his commune's territory every day, and despite the hazards of the journey between his home and Ramallah. Every day, he spends between three and four hours in transit, passing through *checkpoints* and congested roads. Bethlehem is just thirty kilometres from Ramallah.

The other day, Xavier invited me to his home in Beit Jala. After wolfing down a pork burger at the aptly named *Pork Burger*—his favourite fast-food restaurant—he took me to see his family home, located a stone's throw from the vineyards of the Cremisan monastery. The wine produced there is atrocious. But the place is a magnificent vestige of a Palestine that has now disappeared, a country still alive

---

62. Chile is home to the largest Palestinian community outside the Middle East: around 300,000 people.
63. See map p. 94.

in the minds of the old and the imagination of the young, forever imprinted on those magnificent black and white photos from the beginning of the last century: a land of green hills interspersed with pine trees, dirt roads, and old stone houses. Xavier's ancestral home is one of these, lost in the middle of a tiny, unspoilt valley. We approach it on foot from the small forest of Cremisan. The house is only a few dozen meters from us. It's out of reach: the dwelling is now part of an Israeli military zone. Further on, at the Abu Ghneim Hill confiscated by the Har Homa settlement,[64] Israeli cranes are busy. They get closer every day. They will soon come to sully this lost paradise after having emptied it of its few Palestinian inhabitants. In the end, isn't it all just a matter of time?

In the same way, every NSU member's stay in the Palestinian territories remains at the mercy of Israel's goodwill. This applies to Palestinians as well as to those of us with foreign passports. Xavier can no longer return to Palestine—like other advisors in the past, he is blocked in Amman, Jordan.

As is customary, Xavier had left the West Bank to renew his expiring visa—it should be pointed out that the Israeli Ministry of the Interior refuses to grant work permits to NSU employees. All NSU consultants work on tourist visas. They leave the country every three months, keeping their fingers crossed that their residence permits will be renewed on their return. This time, the Israelis did Xavier no favours, and they deported him. He has just been notified that he is

---

64. See map p. 94.

to be put on a plane to Chile. The Chilean ambassadors in Israel and Jordan are still trying to arrange it. For the time being, I have to make do without him.

A national committee for the commemoration of the Nakba has been set up in Ramallah. Despite this, the organization of the celebrations is completely fragmented. It's a pity: civilians and NGOs, both here and in the Diaspora, are particularly active. Initiatives are multiplying. Articles abound in the international press. The battle for public opinion has begun.

The Palestinian Authority, for its part, is wavering. At first, it seemed tempted to organize its own demonstration. We tried to suggest various ideas, but to no avail. The Sulta seems to be at a loss as to what to do next. Finally, the Authority decides to keep a low profile. We receive word that President Abbas will be travelling abroad on 14 and 15 May. So that's it: Abu Mazen, a herald in spite of himself, will be playing his escape act. To crown this sad episode, the head of the PLO will embody exile, far from his own people, on Nakba Day.

*

Given the way events are shaping up, my hopes are quickly being pinned on the article we'd like to see published in the international press on the sixtieth anniversary of the Nakba, Israel's sixtieth birthday. It would be a great media coup. The idea is to put Palestinian refugees back at the centre of the debate, and to explain why it is in the interests of peace and of Israel that the Hebrew state acknowledge its responsibility in creating this problem.

We approached the *New York Times, Le Monde,* and *El País with* a view to publishing the article on 15 May. At the end of a tedious process, the document, reviewed and amended too many times by the NSU and Mahmoud Abbas's advisors, was submitted to the President. He gave the green light—a first success. The authorization came late, but I don't despair; publication can still be envisaged in time.

I have an appointment with Rafic Husseini, Abbas's chief of staff, to settle the final details. The advisor receives me courteously. He wants us to review the text together. He finds the article a little long, its tone a little too legalistic. Some of the words are too sophisticated for his taste. He nitpicks. I'm as accommodating as possible. My goal is to see the article published, but the discussion drags on without me really seeing what he's getting at. Rafic Husseini looks embarrassed.

We've come to the end of our examination of the text. Subject to the few points we've just discussed, he gives me a half-hearted indication that the publication can proceed. Just as I'm about to thank him warmly and rush back to my office, he coolly dismisses me:

'It goes without saying that ^{Dr.} Saeb needs to review this document, doesn't he? Being in charge of negotiations with Israel, I want him to give us his approval too.'

Rafic Husseini stares at me. I remain silent. Abu Mazen's chief of staff doesn't want to take responsibility for publishing the column. Even though the President has agreed in principle, he wants to cover his tracks.

'Naturally,' I reply, with a tense smile.

I leave the room in turmoil: I'm now forced to ask Saeb's approval at the last minute, in a hurry. Fortunately, I had taken the precaution of keeping him informed of the draft article. At least he shouldn't be surprised.

Saeb Erekat is at home. He asked me to send him the text by e-mail. He'll get back to me as soon as he's read it. It's 9pm. I went back to the office to wait feverishly for his call. I had promised the newspapers that I would get back to them before the end of the day's work. For *Le Monde* and *El País*, it's already too late.

My phone rings. I pick it up. Saeb shouts at the other end:

'Ziyad, we can't publish this text. It's out of the question. You can't put the president [Abu Mazen] at the mercy of Zionist organizations just a few days before Bush's visit to Israel and a very important meeting in Sharm El Sheikh. Don't you think the president is fragile enough as it is? Why put him at risk...'

I can hardly contain his flow of words. I interrupt:

'But Doctor, the President has already agreed to the article. The sixtieth anniversary of the Nakba is an opportunity he cannot pass up. It's part of his role to make these statements. It will strengthen him with his people and in the negotiations.'

Saeb Erekat disagrees.

'No, it's too risky. All the American Jewish organizations, Olmert, Livni, the Americans, will come down on us.'

I don't give up. The discussion continues:

'Ziyad, give me forty-eight hours. I'll review the document in more detail, and I'll be able to discuss it with the president this Wednesday.'

'But, Doctor, it will be too late. We've already passed the deadline set by the newspapers.'

We remain silent for a moment. Finally, the chief negotiator speaks again:

'Another solution would be to publish the tribune under my name.'

I can't believe my ears. It doesn't make sense… Saeb isn't even a refugee. I'm disgusted. I tell him I'll think about it. I hang up. In a rage, I kick the wall of my office. The plaster partition gives way; I've made a huge hole in the wall.

The NSU manager discovered the damage the next day. He won't hold it against me, understanding that my irritation was indeed legitimate. Unfortunately, the problem remains: if the PLO refuses to do so, who will promote the rights of Palestinian refugees?

*

On 15 May, as planned, Abu Mazen was not with his people to commemorate the Nakba. All he had to do was make a short visit to a dummy refugee camp built for the occasion opposite the Mukataa, his headquarters in Ramallah. All he had to do was go 500 meters further to find a real camp where he could address his people. For his part, Saeb Erekat issued a simple press release. Just one more.

In Israel, George W Bush delivers a disastrous speech to the Knesset. Disastrous for the Palestinians, of course, and for peace. Disastrous for everyone, in fact, given that Israel's future is intimately entwined with the creation of a Palestinian state. In his glorification of the Hebrew state, the Jewish people and the 'Israeli miracle,' the American president said not a word about the fate and unfulfilled hopes of Israel's Palestinian neighbour. The Sharm El Sheikh summit will not even play the role of a catch-up session. Once again, the PLO feels betrayed. The Palestinian people do too, no doubt.

Shortly before, on 11 May 2008, the PLO signed a relatively indifferent agreement with the Sudanese government and the United Nations High Commissioner for Refugees (UNHCR) to transfer 2,000 Palestinian refugees who had been trapped for many months in miserable conditions on the Syrian–Iraqi border.[65] These Palestinians have won the right to settle in the housing estates of a Khartoum district, created for them a few years ago, named Al Qods. For them, the dreams of return will continue. Under a blazing sun, at the gateway to a new desert. Far, far away from Jerusalem.

Xavier is stuck in a transit zone in Madrid. He is now the PLO representative to Spain who is doing his utmost to try

---

65. Following the fall of Saddam Hussein's regime, the Palestinian refugees who had settled in Iraq since the Nakba were subjected to violence and persecution, leading many of them to flee. With Syria and Jordan refusing to accept new refugees on their territory, several thousand Palestinian refugees were trapped for many months on the Iraqi border, in the desert, awaiting expatriation solutions in third countries.

and enable his return to the West Bank. We are sending messages of support to our colleague. I spoke to him on the phone: he is heartbroken at not being able to return to Palestine prison.

As President Abbas might have written, the Nakba, the 'catastrophe,' continues.[66]

*

I parted ways with Nahla. A heartbreak. But did I really have a choice? My new housekeeper is named Oum Arafat, Arafat's mother—Arafat is her eldest son's name. Good luck to him. Oum Arafat doesn't want to work in my presence, under a man's gaze. Fine—it's certainly not very practical, but at least I'm sure I won't have to deal with another momentary lapse on the part of my housekeeper.

Oum Arafat has come to tidy up the apartment with her daughter. The little girl must be barely twelve years of age. I'm sorry to see her wasting the day at my place, working with her mother. Oum Arafat and her family live in Beitunia[67] on the outskirts of Ramallah, so at the end of their working day, I offer to drive them home.

The two women sat in the back of my car. It's a pleasant little ride. The sun is shining brightly. After dropping off the mother and daughter, I set off on the return journey. I drive quietly, distractedly, towards Ramallah. The musician

---

66. The draft op-ed, to which President Mahmoud Abbas agreed for publication on 15 May 2008, is reproduced in Appendix III.
67. See map p. 94.

on the radio sings at the top of its lungs. I barely notice a car nipping at my heels. It nearly crashes into me before I notice. The driver comes up to me. He's agitated. He accelerates suddenly to overtake me. He swerves violently to the right, cutting me off. I brake on with all my might to avoid an accident. I end up a hair's breadth from his bumper.

The man gets out of his car. He comes to meet me. He's nervous. I'm very upset. The collision was narrowly averted. He greets me:

'As-salamu alaikum.'

I don't reply. He repeats his greetings, which I don't return.

'What's your problem? You almost ran into me!' My anger wins out.

'Where are you from?'

'I asked you a question. I'm asking why you almost hit my car.'

'I asked you where you were from.'

'None of your business. What's your problem?'

'I want to see your ID.'

I stare at my interlocutor. The man is in his early forties. His moustache gives him a semblance of authority. But he looks feverish and tense. He's sweating profusely. His hands are trembling.

I fix my stare at him, pretending not to understand. Without taking his eyes off me, he puts his hand under his jacket and rests it on a pistol hanging from his belt. He unsubtly shows me his gun. I understand immediately: Mukhabarat. The kamikaze driver belongs to Palestinian intelligence. I declare my identity. Better still, amused, I take out my business card. The plainclothes agent takes note of it:

Ziyad Clot
Legal Advisor
Negotiations Department
Palestine Liberation Organization

A little viciously, I add that I work for Dr Saeb Erekat. The poor guy is confused. The plainclothes officer apologizes profusely. He greets me and takes his leave in an instant.

I remain parked until I recover my senses. I take a look in the on-board mirror to see how I look. Unshaven for three days, my hair could do with a trim too. With my pair of dark aviator-style glasses, I look like Ali Hassan Salameh[68] of Force 17, Arafat's private security in Lebanon. It's a PLO-style look that harkens back to the *70s*, the Munich generation. In short, I look like a terrorist. Today, Fatah has a much cleaner and acceptable style.

I tell a few NSU colleagues about my adventure. I confirm that the hunt for 'terrorists'—Islamists, these days—is on in the West Bank more than ever. Hizb ut-Tahrir, the liberation

---

68. Born in 1940 in Lydda, Ali Hassan Salameh joined Fatah in the 1960s and later created Force 17 in Beirut, Yasser Arafat's bodyguard. He is also regarded as the main instigator of the hostage-taking of Israeli athletes at the 1972 Munich Olympics. He later became one of the CIA's privileged contacts in Lebanon. Salameh was killed in a car explosion on 22 January 1979, as part of Israel's secret 'Wrath of God' operation to eliminate those responsible for the bloody Munich massacre.

party, is planning a large rally in Ramallah. President Abbas's security forces are on high alert. The demonstration has been banned. Hizb ut-Tahrir advocates the establishment of a caliphate that would rule the entire Arab world, including Palestine—the whole of Palestine, that is—into which the 'Zionist entity' would disintegrate. It holds a vast mandate, scarcely more unrealistic than the search for a territorial compromise between Israelis and Palestinians.

I almost forgot to mention that the border discussions have become somewhat more concrete, but that doesn't mean progress is being made. The Palestinian delegation in charge of the territorial question has been ordered to put a map on the table. They continue to act in the hope of seeing these negotiations unblocked. I confess that I'm following these tortuous talks, reported to me by my associates, with increasing distance. The negotiations, the two-state solution, the Palestinian state in the West Bank and Gaza Strip with East Jerusalem as its capital: I don't believe in them anymore.

IX

NEGOTIATIONS
JUNE / SEPTEMBER 2008

Six months since the peace talks began—despite the Israeli wait-and-see attitude at the negotiating table, despite the activism of their shovels and army in the territories, despite Palestinian division and frustration, one meeting follows another in West Jerusalem hotels.

The general structure of the Israeli–Palestinian peace treaty has already been prepared by the parties. But, in the absence of agreement on its content, it remains an empty shell. The Palestinians face an unshakable wall. To make matters worse, the Kadima party, which includes Prime Minister Ehud Olmert and Foreign Minister Tzipi Livni, intends to hold its primaries in September. Olmert is caught up in politics, and Livni will soon return to the campaign trail. Barring a miracle over the summer, it's all over. There will be no agreement.

Yet written proposals on refugees continue to be exchanged between Saeb Erekat and Tal Becker. My instructions are to try to bring the respective drafts of the article on refugees closer together, 'without compromising

Palestinian positions,' Saeb directs. Even if we don't agree on anything, we must give the impression that the parties are moving closer together. The PLO, the Israeli government, the Americans, and the EU need to keep this illusion alive. Despite my insistence, Saeb refuses to let me brief him on the refugees.

Condoleezza Rice had left the parties relatively free to talk during the first months of the year. Now she's dialling up the pressure. She accompanied President Bush on his official visit last May, and she returns a month later to take stock of the talks.

We're trying to convince Abu Alaa and Saeb Erekat that it's now essential to send Rice a letter outlining our fears associated with the continuation of Israel's fait accompli in the occupied territories and clarifying Palestinian positions to account for their moderation. We're already halfway through 2008, the year in which the creation of a Palestinian state is supposed to take place. Either we're still hoping for an agreement and need to find a way of forcing the Israelis to show a modicum of flexibility, or we've taken for granted the slow but sure deflagration of the peace process, in which case we need to anticipate future Israeli attempts to blame the failure of negotiations on the PLO. This letter would kill two birds with one stone. The missive is ready for Rice's new visit on 15 June.[69]

I'm away in Europe for most of June. Although I'm in daily contact with Ramallah, I'm not unhappy to finally

---

69. Read the draft letter from the Palestinian delegation to Condoleezza Rice reproduced in Appendix IV.

be able to take a step back. It's more gratifying to promote Palestinian positions abroad, as I'm doing now, than on the front line, where I tolerate the limitations, fragility, and compromises of the PLO and Israel's 'to the limit' attitude. I first accompanied Maen Areikat, vice president of the PLO's negotiations department, to meetings in Paris. These were held prior to Nicolas Sarkozy's forthcoming official visit to Israel and the Palestinian territories. I then went to London for a meeting of experts on the refugee issue. These meetings were positive.

On 16 June, however, the Palestinians suffered a violent setback on the European diplomatic front. The EU agreed to enhance its partnership relations with Israel, ignoring European demands for respect for human rights. Palestinian Authority Prime Minister Salam Fayyad had sent a letter to all European decision-makers to raise the issue. The document, prepared by the NSU, angered Ehud Olmert. I was ready to go and hammer the point home in Brussels in support of Palestine's representation there, but the NSU manager discouraged me: 'too sensitive,' he said, too risky for the continuation of the Adam Smith project in the occupied territories. We passed the buck. Negotiating under occupation has limits that I still haven't grasped: the Israelis could force NSU out of business tomorrow if they want to.

The *upgrade of* relations with Israel has, of course, been adopted. For the time being, the Europeans, led by Sarkozy's France, have convinced themselves that, by developing a privileged relationship with the Jewish state, they will be able to have a greater influence on the peace process and Israel's policy towards the Palestinians. If it's the Israeli–American relationship they're taking as a model, that's promising.

I learnt a bit later that France wanted to work on a proposal to be made to Israel and the PLO over the course of the summer. The feeling on the French side is that the end of George W Bush's mandate will mean a gradual disengagement of the American administration. French diplomacy, leading the European Council for six months, does not want to let such a great opportunity pass. The Quai d'Orsay intends to draw up an offer that would keep the negotiations alive and ensure the implementation of an eventual agreement. Apparently, they still believe in it.

I'll pass on the message when I get back to Ramallah. The French want to discuss their approach with Abu Mazen and his advisors at the Union for the Mediterranean summit scheduled for 12 and 13 July in Paris. The PLO is not listening. Once again, the Palestinians in Ramallah seem determined to put all their eggs in one basket, that of Uncle Sam. Pity. This augurs further disappointments.

However, I have no illusions about the political line taken by the Élysée on the Israeli–Palestinian conflict. Like Bush, Sarkozy affirmed before the Knesset his unconditional support for the 'Jewish people' and praised the 'Israeli miracle.'[70] However, unlike the American president, he had one brief but essential word to say on the need to create a Palestinian state with East Jerusalem as its capital.

---

70. Speech dated 23 June 2008: http://www.diplomatie.gouv.fr/fr/article_imprim.php3?id_article=63849.

*

Unsurprisingly, the meetings held in Jerusalem with the Israelis and Americans in the second half of June are inconclusive. This is not enough to convince Abu Alaa and Saeb Erekat of the need to hand over the letter prepared by the NSU to Rice. Nevertheless, the American Secretary of State seems aware that there remains a long way to go. The clock is ticking. In a few weeks' time, the United States will have to report on the outcome of the Annapolis negotiations.

For the moment, discussions are still stalled over borders—and everything else. The PLO has, however, resigned itself to accepting for the first time that certain settlements will not be dismantled and will become part of Israel's future borders. This may not be something to celebrate, but it's historic, if nothing else. The Palestinians have put a card on the table: they are ready to accept that the settlements of French Hill, Ramat Eshkol, Ramot Alon, Ramat Shlomo, Gilo, and Talpiot[71] pass to Israel, in addition to the Jewish quarter of Jerusalem's Old City. This offer would include 70 per cent of the settlers in the Jewish state.

For Livni, this is not enough. The head of Israeli diplomacy is demanding that her country's sovereignty also extend to Ma'ale Adumim, Ephrat, Ariel, Pisgat Zeev, and Har Homa. Now in election season, Livni is even more inflexible than usual, which is really saying a lot.

---

71. See map p. 94.

The parties meet again at Jerusalem's *King David* Hotel on 30 June. Abu Alaa tries to put the issue of Jerusalem back on the table. Livni plays dumb:

'Since I can't talk about it, I won't say anything. I'll just listen.'

Apparently, she has just been informed that the Knesset has passed its first reading of a law requiring any transfer of territories annexed by Israel to be subject to a referendum. Abou Alaa asks about the state of Israeli opinion.

'Will the Israelis vote to return the Golan to Syria?' he asks.
'No. Even if the Golan does not belong to what we call the "Land of Israel," the majority of Israelis do not want to give it back to Syria. This law also applies to Jerusalem.'

The Palestinian recalls his approach, even more accommodating than the one supported by law and the international community:

'Jerusalem has been part of the occupied territories since 1967. We can discuss and agree on many issues related to Jerusalem: holy sites, infrastructure, the municipality, economic issues, security, settlements. But for us, the borders of the municipality of Jerusalem are those of 1967. That's the basis, and we have to start from there.'

Livni remained silent. She closes the discussion with a quip:

'Houston, we have a problem.'

I don't like this turn of events at all. The Israelis are now using domestic politics as a pretext to justify their intransigence. This luxury is not afforded to the Palestinians, who could use the same pretext of politics to thwart diplomatic efforts: the internal Palestinian split, the population's growing discontent with the Sulta, the Gaza blockade, the explosion of settlements in the West Bank... The only problem is that we need to show progress in the talks, and Mahmoud Abbas's PLO has made negotiations its business. We can keep ourselves busy: as the Israelis go about their business, it's the Americans who are going to make themselves available in their place. Rice seems to have gotten it into her head to see what can be achieved in Ramallah. No doubt she'll be pulling out all the stops in the run-up to the next UN General Assembly in September.

Rice has the refugees in her sights. She believes that an agreement is possible on this issue, but only if the Palestinians follow her instructions: the PLO must give in on the issue of recognizing Israel's responsibility in creating and perpetuating the problem. Despite sixty years of dispossession and exile, she believes that Palestinian refugees have no right to reparations for the non-material damage they have suffered. You must know how to look ahead. For Rice, the Palestinians must see the creation of a state as the best form of compensation. I find it hard to see how a definitive amputation of almost 80 per cent of historically Palestinian territory can constitute a form of compensation for the Palestinian people. The American diplomat nevertheless seems convinced of the soundness of her analysis. Finally, she wants to define how the international community can help on this issue and will ask her advisors to look into the matter. Saeb Erekat told her that the NSU had already done a lot of work on this. I'm told that we'll be meeting an advisor from the US State Department, a certain Jonathan Schwartz, in the coming weeks. From now on, I'm in their sights too.

*

July arrives. A Palestinian worker has had enough and drives a front-end loader into traffic, impaling it on a bus full of passengers on Jaffa Street, in the heart of Jerusalem. The impact killed three people. The worker is shot at point-blank range by Israeli police and Jerusalem plunges into shock. A state of emergency is declared.

The perpetrator of the attack left no word, no clue to explain his act. The Israeli security services are desperately trying to identify the murderer's motives: a criminal record, affiliation with Hamas or other 'hardline' Palestinian movements, but they can find nothing. Yet you don't have to be Einstein to understand the trajectory of the Palestinian who decides to kill himself: can a Palestinian worker who, in order to survive, works on the construction of Jewish settlements on his own land, which is slipping further and further out from under his feet, remain mentally healthy?

I was summoned to the American consulate in East Jerusalem on 8 July. Rice's wishes are granted; I am asked to present the NSU's work on the international mechanism for resolving the fate of Palestinian refugees.[72] There's no

---

72. Ever since the first negotiations on Palestinian refugees in the 1990s, the idea has taken hold that an international mechanism would be needed to resolve the issue. This agency would be in charge of implementing the return and "relocation" of refugees, their rights to compensation, their rehabilitation, and so on.

doubt that the Americans want to play a leading role on this issue but are acting in support of Israeli interests. For them, it's a question of facilitating an agreement on refugees that would be the least costly possible for the Jewish state.

If it weren't for the fact that I'm endorsing disastrous diplomatic policies, I'd readily admit that it's rather pleasant to visit the American consulate. In fact, I go there quite often. Of course, I come across more and more cranes and works-in-progress, and I try to ignore the bulldozers, of which there are many. But the consulate occupies a beautiful location in West Jerusalem, opposite a lovely park, where I park my car, always in the same place. I do the same today, except this time I notice some graves at the far end of the park, by the side of the road. Their presence intrigues me. I can make out Arabic inscriptions on the graves. They seem doomed to abandonment.

My meeting at the American consulate went well—things are just beginning to get serious for me. Palestinian despair, on the other hand, runs its course. A second bulldozer driver went mad on the outskirts of the Holy City. On 22 July, another Palestinian drove his vehicle into one bus and at least two cars. Three victims are in critical condition, and a dozen others were minorly injured. Like the other attacker, the perpetrator of this tragedy is neither a politician nor a fanatic, nor will he be given the opportunity to reflect on his deed—he was shot dead on the spot.

On the Palestinian side, terrorism used to be a political act. Since the second Intifada, it had taken on religious overtones. Today, it has become the crudest expression of despair.

I try not to agonize too much, despite the terroristic bulldozers, despite the vain pursuit of negotiations, maintained by the Americans. If only it were just a waste of time and money. I'm afraid it's much more serious: at the rate things are going, the 'peace process,' combined with Israel's policy of fait accompli, risks crushing the last Palestinian demands one by one.

I can't just stand by. Saeb has a mind of his own and won't share even a shred of information about the negotiations with the refugee organizations. Nevertheless, I decide to inform a few trustworthy people of the essentials. I absolutely must prevent a twisted coup by the Americans, the Israelis, the PLO. I have suggested to my contacts that they mobilize refugee organizations to make their views known to the Palestinian Authority as quickly as possible. The Sulta must be accountable for the direction of its negotiations with Israel. The individual rights of Palestinian refugees must be respected.

My initiative is risky. I'm overstepping my mandate as NSU's legal advisor—but I have no choice. Perhaps it's an expression of my own desperation. Or maybe it's my way of putting up a resistance.

Until now, the Israelis at least agreed to meet us. That's no longer the case. So we meet amongst ourselves, as part of the Palestinian negotiating delegation. The other side doesn't want to meet us? That doesn't stop us, as Saeb asks us to draw up the agreement on our own, detailing our positions and specifying those of the Israelis, where possible. Saeb and Abu Alaa take the document to Washington. The idea is to deliver the draft treaty with the letter to Rice,

There Will Be No Palestinian State

which is still pending. So here we go again. Except that refugees are now at the centre of the debate.

The delegation returned from the US a few days later. The discussions held there were far from brilliant, but no decisions were finalized. That's already something. The draft letter to Rice was definitively buried by Abu Alaa and Saeb. They didn't want to 'offend' their American 'ally.' Too bad for the PLO. Likewise, the 'unilateral' agreement was postponed. It makes no sense whatsoever. I wonder how the Americans understood by this. Meanwhile, Olmert announced that no *deal* regarding Jerusalem could be expected this year. Rice, for her part, desperately needs an agreement, even a partial one; she needs something to sink her teeth into.

On 29 July, the head of American diplomacy declare that settlement construction was a 'problem'—what a revelation. Even Abu Alaa, an old-school Palestinian nationalist, is finally accepting the obvious. Noting that the Israelis are still unwilling to recognize the 1967 borders, he told the press that the Palestinians will soon have to come to terms with their demand for integration into a bi-national state. Coming from the head of the Palestinian negotiating delegation, the statement caused quite a stir.

*

The moment arrives like a foregone conclusion. Although Saeb makes it clear that the meeting he's inviting me to attend is not a negotiating session, I know that the process is now underway. I have a feeling I'm going to have to assist Saeb in his forthcoming discussions on refugees. It's the middle of August. The rights of Palestinian refugees are about to give rise to unprecedented sales. And fate has chosen me as the instrument of this great liquidation.

Act One: *King David* Hotel, Jerusalem, 14 August 2008. Opposite us, a delegation of three seemingly friendly people: Tal Becker, Livni's chief of staff, a certain Daniel Taub who assists her, and a third person, a young lawyer.

I'm here to present the Palestinian vision of the international mechanism, already discussed at my meeting at the American Consulate. This presentation is the fruit of several years' work by the NSU with various international experts. All eyes are on me. My computer takes a long time to load. I'm tempted to say something to keep them waiting. Like, 'This is a Palestinian computer.' But maybe that's not such a good idea—let's avoid it. The presentation finally appears on my screen. 'Palestinian refugees, PowerPoint version.' I start.

The Israelis are attentive. They take notes. They interrupt me with comments. I seem to be doing pretty well. Saeb also asks questions. The meeting ends after about an hour. The Israelis are now informed of the work being done on the Palestinian side on this vital issue. It's something. When you're Palestinian, you learn to be satisfied with small victories.

A few days later, Hamas issued a statement. The Islamist movement suspected the Sulta of selling out the right of return within the future Palestinian state. It's a bit of a caricature, but not unfounded. The truth is that ever since

I arrived at the NSU, I've been unable to determine the red lines of Abu Mazen and his followers. How far are they prepared to give in on the refugee issue to get their way? Are they willing to give up the right of return in exchange for their state? I can't rule it out.

It was Sari Nusseibeh,[73] who a few years ago, together with his Israeli counterpart Ami Ayalon, augured this dark prospect of giving up the right of return for refugees in exchange for the establishment of a Palestine with East Jerusalem as its capital. Before that, in the early 1980s, Nusseibeh had been one of the first to embrace the two-state solution. Each time he brought it up, he drew the wrath of his compatriots, who accused him of treason. If his career bears witness to the slow but inevitable erosion of Palestinian positions, today, fifteen years after the Oslo Accords, Nusseibeh believes that the viability of the two-state solution has come to an end. For him, Israelis and Palestinians are letting their last chance slip away.

He believes it is now time for the PLO to modernize. The Palestinians must reconsider the idea of a single state for all, and fight peacefully for equal rights within that state, as in South Africa. The process promises to be long, perilous, and difficult. The Palestinians and Israelis do not prefer this choice, but the other options have been exhausted.

I couldn't agree more.

---

73. Sari Nusseibeh is Professor of Philosophy and President of Al Quds University in Jerusalem. He is also a Palestinian politician renowned for his 'moderate' positions. He is the author of a best-selling autobiography: *Il était un pays. Une vie en Palestine*, Paris, Lattès, 2008.

Like a sign of fate, Mahmoud Darwish died on 19 August. He had drafted the 1988 declaration of Palestinian independence, in which the PLO resigned itself to living side by side with the Israelis on just 22 per cent of the land of historic Palestine. Palestine is in mourning.

Sadly, the funeral of the author of exile was taken over by PLO caciques. The Palestinian poet from Galilee, who dreamed of returning to his native village, now in Israel, will be buried in Ramallah. The PLO did not insist that Darwish be laid to rest in Al-Birwa, where his mother still lives. The official funeral will take place at Mukataa, the Sulta headquarters in Ramallah. Mahmoud Abbas and his security forces, Mahmoud Dahlan and the American generals, diplomats in large numbers, are there to honour the poet's soul. That's what I'm told. Although I am invited to attend his funeral with my NSU colleagues, I don't go. I don't belong there. Nor do the thousands of anonymous Darwish readers who were not invited.

*

For act II: the French enter the scene. They want to put their paper on the table in the name of Europe. As usual, the PLO was unprepared. Saeb, anxious not to jeopardize his relationship with the American administration, would not hear of the initiative. Nevertheless, on 20 August, a diplomat from the French consulate was asked to present the offer. I attended the meeting, at the end of which Saeb made it clear that he would not accept any official response. He nevertheless asked the NSU to prepare its comments on the proposal with the utmost discretion. I was asked to coordinate this work.

As I prepare to leave his office, Saeb beckons me to remain seated. With an air of calm, he praises my work. Then, almost martial, he asks me if I'd like to join him at the next refugee negotiation meeting. The request was expected. The message is clear. I'm faced with my responsibilities: either I refuse, and Saeb Erekat goes off on his own to discuss the dossier with Tal Becker. Or I accept, and Saeb will at least have my technical expertise at his disposal. I'll also be in a position to keep abreast of developments in the discussions with the Israelis. I'm of the opinion that the epilogue to this round of negotiations is not far off. My aim will be to do my best to hold the Palestinian positions.

My answer is yes.

I've done it. I've crossed the Rubicon. I've crossed over to the negotiating side.

Maen Areikat, also present, adds, 'Sleep well Ziyad, it won't be a cakewalk.'

I meet up with Saeb on 24 August. We have a big day ahead of us. It begins with a visit to the French Consulate in Jerusalem. Consul Alain Rémy has had to cut short his vacation in France. He has been urgently dispatched to sell France's 'European' proposal.

The meeting soon turns sour. Saeb explains that before their meeting in the United States, he and Livni had agreed to reject any third-party interference in their discussions. Saeb does not spare his French interlocutor. The French offer leaves much to be desired, it's true; it suggests certain solutions in violation of international law, such as compensation for Israeli settlers who will have to be transferred to Israel. The EU would offer to pay for 40 years of settlements instead of Israel. Saeb finds it hard to swallow. The consul insists: it's essential to keep the peace process alive in the run-up to the US presidential election. The Palestinian negotiator doesn't give in:

'We are not going to prevent France from presenting its offer. It's just that we have decided with the Israelis to protect ourselves from a new Camp David scenario. If there were no Kadima elections, the Israelis would show more commitment.' He continues, 'I'm not going to change my alliances. I need to maintain my credibility. You cannot, as France, deviate from international law. If the price to pay is to distance yourself from international law, I don't want you. I need a deal that can defeat Hamas and give me 70 per cent of the Palestinian vote.'

Saeb singles me out in a friendly tone. He wants me to share my opinion with my compatriots. I give a Norman reply. Saeb softens his tone:

'I want to talk to Kouchner. The three of us have to meet. I have a confidential proposal that I want to share with him. I'm going to discuss it today with Tal Becker [...] It won't be possible to reach a full agreement before November because of the situation in Israel. There are three possible scenarios:

1. A "Camp David" scenario: we say no. We refuse an agreement because it does not satisfy our interests. This would be another collapse of the peace process. I won't let that happen again. This experience has been far too painful for my people in the recent past.

2. Continue to discuss and make our best efforts to try to achieve something by the end of the year.

3. The alternative I propose is to keep alive the objectives announced at Annapolis. By November, the situation in Israel will have calmed down. Livni and I will meet with Kouchner to develop a matrix.'[74]

He insists on the extremely confidential nature of this last proposal. The consul looks relieved. We leave the consulate lounge. Saeb makes no secret of his satisfaction. He's happy with his move. He was on the verge being reprimanded by the French, but it should be said that he handled the meeting well. As for the overall strategy, however, I'm far from convinced.

Saeb and I set off again. Tal Becker is waiting for us at the nearby *Inbal* Hotel. This time, he's alone. Round-faced, with a small yarmulke on his head, he greets Saeb warmly. Then he greets me politely. This is my second meeting with the Israelis. This time, I'm not here as an expert—I'm a negotiator, unbelievably. But it's been a long time since the best Palestinian minds, our most experienced professionals, wanted to hear any more about the 'peace process.' They distanced themselves from the PLO long ago. We need look no further for the reason why Saeb Erekat is joined in this room by me, a French lawyer in his early thirties, who first set foot in Palestine barely a year ago.

---

74. The idea is to seal the Israeli and Palestinian positions in a document to be kept by the USA and France that could be passed on to the next American administration in the hope of resuming talks.

Saeb began by informing Tal of the plan discussed with the French: if no agreement is reached before the end of the year, a table showing the positions of both sides will be given to the Americans and the French, in the hope of resuming negotiations in 2009. Tal agrees in principle, on condition that it remains strictly confidential. He adds that Condoleezza Rice is under pressure and is likely to do everything in her power to force an agreement before the end of President Bush's term of office.

The Israeli negotiator then makes his personal comments on the work we have presented on the international mechanism. He calmly explains why he has a problem with our vision. I take note of his remarks and wait for him to finish before replying point by point.

It's very hot in this room. Tal is starting to sweat. Saeb has also taken out his handkerchief to mop his brow. The Israeli gets up to turn the air-conditioning back on. The discussion quickly turns to Israel's responsibility for creating the refugee problem. The Israeli War of Independence clashes with the Palestinian Nakba. Inevitably, things get out of hand:

'Acknowledgement of responsibility is a bilateral issue. I don't want the Americans involved in this discussion,' Saeb begins.

Tal responds, 'Our respective histories cannot be reconciled. You think you're the victims. We think *we* are the victims.'

'How can you seriously think that you are the victims of the Israeli–Palestinian conflict?'

'Arab armies invaded us. The Arabs never accepted the partition plan. Your problem, Saeb, and the problem of the

Palestinians and the Arab countries, is that you still don't recognize us as a people, the Jewish people. Judaism is not just a religion. First and foremost, we are a people.'

Saeb grows irritated. The air conditioning has crashed again. I try to bring some order to the discussion:

'Very well, then. Let's consider for a moment that the respective histories of what may have happened in 1947 to 1948 are irreconcilable—which I don't think they are, but let's move on. I have two comments:

First, the question of Israeli responsibility for the fate of the Palestinian refugees cuts across two aspects: the refugees were forced to leave their homes—let's put the reasons for this exile aside for the moment. Secondly, Palestinians have been prevented from returning to their homes. Can Israel reasonably dispute that concrete legal measures were taken to prevent the return of Palestinian refugees after 1948? Various Knesset laws have recognized and implemented the confiscation of refugee land. The State of Israel has refused to give Palestinian refugees Israeli citizenship, etc. These laws were passed and are still in force. They are in complete contradiction with international law. Can Israel reasonably continue to deny these facts?

What's more, the international community can also be seen as bearing some responsibility for the creation and unresolved refugee problem. Do you think Israel could consider recognizing a shared responsibility with the international community? Would this facilitate the terms of our discussion?'

Tal glares at me. He doesn't answer. He wants to get back to the agenda, which he says is the international mechanism. Saeb agrees. Tal tries to stick me on one or two technical questions in passing. Livni's chief of staff continues, this time with a straight face:

'To put it simply, I think your vision [of the mechanism] is unrealistic. My view is that work on the mechanism should be conducted with the following factors in mind: what can be sold to Israelis and Palestinians, what can be offered by the international community, and what works in practice. Israel will not agree to participate in a mechanism where it will have to run the risk of facing the veto of other countries—Syria, for example.'

Saeb wants to return to the article on refugees. He wants to focus on the document that will be included in the agreement. For months, the two men have been trying to isolate the purely political issues that will ultimately be decided by Olmert and Abbas. As the exchanges progress, however, the question inevitably returns to the heart of the matter *via* the debate on the international mechanism. Tal wants to impose US leadership on the resolution of the problem:

'Why not the UN?' asks Saeb.
'We don't trust the UN,' replies Tal.

I set out in detail my technical and political reservations about possible American leadership of the mechanism. Tal continues to say that he cannot accept any reference to the principle of full compensation for Palestinian refugees. Restitution of their property? Don't dream. That's 'naturally' out of the question, he asserts. Yet these are the rights of Palestinian refugees under applicable international law. Tal sidesteps the issue.

There Will Be No Palestinian State

The discussion must end. Saeb announces that he is expected in Ramallah for the launch of his book: *Life is a negotiation.* I think it's a joke, but it's not. Tal Becker concludes the meeting:

'Let's sum it up. We have made good progress: in particular, the Israelis are ready to accept the structure of the article you have proposed. However, we must remain aware of the risk of creating expectations that we won't be able to meet.'

I have to make do with these crumbs to keep up appearances. There's nothing, really nothing, to be gained from the Israelis. I can't wait for these meetings to stop. End of act II.

*

I'm now immersed in the action. It's not just a feeling, it's real: the twinge in my heart and the ache in my stomach bear witness to it. I'm preparing myself for the prospect of a lively third round. Things should settle down. The Americans—Rice and her advisors—are back. The French have not given up. Further meetings will follow with Saeb and Tal. I work a lot; I don't sleep much.

Our meeting with Jonathan Schwartz, US legal advisor on Israeli–Palestinian issues, will take place at NSU. He will meet us there on 26 August, after his meetings in Jerusalem with Rice and company. Schwartz knows his stuff: he was already on the job at the time of the Camp David negotiations back in 2000.

American security arrives early. Shaven-headed thugs, equipped with earpieces and sunglasses, inspect every nook and cranny of our offices. Schwartz arrives shortly afterwards, accompanied by the American consulate's political advisor. The US State Department official is a clear-eyed, athletic-looking man in his early fifties.

Schwartz has been instructed by Rice to prepare a paper on the international mechanism. He is here to discuss the issue with us. The meeting goes on for almost three hours. The smallest details of the mechanism are scrutinized, in an atmosphere that is always polite and constructive.

Schwartz thanks us at the end of our long discussion. He adds that he appreciates the quality of our work and our commitment, given the pressure on the PLO these days, especially on the refugee issue. It sounds sincere. We're about to take a break before moving on to the discussion on borders, when Schwartz calls out to me:

'The Secretary of State has asked me to warn you: we don't want the French to play any role in the refugee issue. We know they want to stick their noses into the negotiations. That is out of the question.'

His translucent gaze stays on me, as though gauging my reaction. I suppose the fact that I'm French makes me the prime suspect. He has a point—just as he's giving me his warning, I have the document containing the NSU's comments on the French offer in my bag under the table. Everyone looks at me. I get away with a quip,

'Oh, you know *Frenchies*, they're always looking to get noticed...'

We get up from the table to take a breather. I pass the NSU manager in the corridor, who asks me to follow him into his office. He's eager to be debriefed on the meeting. But that's not all, at the end of my debriefing, he signals to me with his hand: he wishes to continue the rest of the discussion in another room. There, he tells me in a whisper that the French are more pressing about their proposal. They absolutely want our commentary. Saeb finally agrees to give it to them, on condition that any trace of him is removed from the document. I learn that our note is currently being modified to meet his conditions. I'm in charge of taking it to the French that evening. My boss asks me to go to Jerusalem after the meeting with the Americans. Before that, he wants me to call the French consul, who has an appointment with Kouchner the next morning in Paris, to reassure him. He hands me his cell phone to make the call. This device would not be bugged.

I return to the meeting room as if nothing had happened. After another protracted meeting, I drive to East Jerusalem to hand over the document to a French diplomat. I chose a small, out-of-the-way hotel to hand over the envelope. East Jerusalem is a nest of spies. What's more, the Americans are in town.

We meet Jonathan Schwartz again the next morning at the American Consulate for a shorter meeting. On this occasion, we give him the peace treaty we have prepared. He's a little surprised. Apparently, he was unaware of the document, which had been given to Rice in Washington. He flips through it, stopping on the last page. He points to the place where the agreement is to be initialled. With a smile on his face, he questions the NSU:

'Am I to understand that the treaty will be signed only by the PLO?'

We all look at each other, looking a little foolish. My fears are confirmed—sending this document without further explanation was a poor idea. At best, we came across as a delegation of inflexible negotiators. At worst, we came across as a bunch of jokers who refuse to consider the Israeli side's point of view, however obtuse it may be.

*

We meet the Israelis again at the *King David* Hotel, barely 24 hours later. After a few agreed-upon words about Jonathan Schwartz's professionalism and our meetings with him, Tal Becker distils his good points and advice:

'I'm very pleased with the efforts on both sides. But we need to remain cautious, because we're creating expectations as our work progresses.'

I support her comments and worry that, according to Schwartz, Rice thinks the parties are now in agreement on 90 per cent of refugee issues. Tal agrees. He adds:

'Rice shows a lack of knowledge of the issues. This is true for Jerusalem. It's also true for the refugees.'

Discussions resumed on the drafting of the famous article to be included in the peace treaty. Each of these meetings is short. An hour, an hour and a half at the most. For Tal and Saeb, it's business as usual. I think they've already met over two hundred times since the beginning of the year. A new date is set for Sunday, 30 August. Ramadan will have begun. Saeb demands that the food be removed from the meeting table. He can already see the Islamists reproaching him for feasting with the Zionists in the middle of the Muslim fast. Tal suggests we meet after sunset. Saeb agrees.

We meet again two days later. Inevitably, we return to the mechanism that crystallizes Israeli–Palestinian differences. Both sides are trapped in their refusal to tackle the heart of the matter. Let me come back to our reservations about possible American leadership on this issue. Saeb goes on to clarify his state of mind:

'I'm not saying no to US leadership. But it would still have to be defined, and I would need guarantees. I don't want to alienate anyone. We met with the French. The European Union could offer its financial contribution. The parties can agree on the entity that will pilot the mechanism: the PLO, the United States, and Israel will decide. I know Ziyad's opinion, but I'll have to get Abu Mazen's decision on this. You have to understand that we're under enormous pressure, especially on this issue.'

The negotiator from Jericho seems to have finally taken the measure of what's at stake. I have the impression that my work is beginning to bear fruit. Tal tries to cajole his Palestinian interlocutor:

'Saeb, you can handle the pressure.'

'Maybe I can. But think of the others.'

'Let me explain what our concern is here. The burden on us [regarding the refugee issue] is too heavy. We will not play an active role in the mechanism. The United States will take the lead.'

Tal decided to push the envelope a little further today. He reveals an open secret that has been kept under wraps until now. He explains that the text of the article on Palestinian refugees must include at least one implicit reference to the future settlement of the fate of Jewish refugees.[75] I'm only too happy to finally be able to engage in this long-awaited discussion. But Saeb stops me dead in my tracks. He rants:

'The question of Jewish refugees has no place in this text! Don't load the boat, Tal. Don't play this game with me...'

In the end, both parties agree that each will update a new version of the article for the next meeting. We put our notes away. Saeb has already taken his cell phone in hand. We are about to take our leave when Tal turns to me:

'Ziyad, really, there's never been such a thorough discussion of this refugee issue. My feeling is that Palestinian refugees have never been so well defended. Sincerely, Ziyad, your work is making a real difference.'

He smiles at me.

I look at Saeb. He looks up from his cell phone.

I'm not sure what Tal Becker is getting at. I'm not particularly interested in making friends with the Israeli negotiator. I'm suspicious. He continues:

---

75. Following the creation of Israel, hundreds of thousands of Jews living in Arab countries were stripped of their property and original nationality. Most of them joined the new state.

'No, frankly, when I see that, I think I'd like to be a Palestinian refugee.'

His reflection leaves me speechless. I'm stunned. My answer comes only after a long silence:

'I can't believe you actually said that.'

Tal Becker also takes a moment to realize the enormous insensitivity of his words. He recovers:

'I was just kidding. I'm sorry.'

We get back in the car with Saeb for Ramallah. As usual, he's on the phone. And as usual, it's with a journalist. On several occasions since I've worked with him, I've tried to talk to him to get a feel for his character. Difficult undertaking, as the negotiator is always between appointments. The man is always on the run. To me, it's a race into the void. For him, it's a marathon: the pursuit of peace is a calling that never lets up.

Saeb has just hung up his phone. He is weary. We're driving past a field of olive trees that has been razed to the ground by the Israeli army. I try my luck:

'I found Tal's comments at the end of the meeting unacceptable...'
'Because you find everything else acceptable?'

Saeb points to the hundreds of tree trunks cut off at the roots. He continues:

'Ziyad, don't kid yourself. We don't have the means to fight the Israelis. We throw stones at them; they send their tanks. We take up arms; they send in their F-16s. They're too strong—they're brutes. As a politician, I can't take the risk of another Intifada. The second uprising left 5,000 dead [on the Palestinian side]. I can't afford another Camp David and all that followed. All we have left are our brains and our ability to convince the Israelis that an agreement is essential for them.'

His mobile rings again. It won't stop ringing until we arrive in Ramallah.

*

As planned, we meet again with the Israelis on 31 August after sunset. This is our fourth meeting. I can't really see any clearer—all I know is that we're on the wrong track. Tal is once again accompanied by Daniel Taub. Each delegation reviews the article prepared by the other, which is supposed to reflect the state of our discussions.

Tal, once again, is self-congratulatory, 'I think we've made a lot of progress. The following issues still divide us: liability, return, restitution, and compensation...'

In short, everything remains to be negotiated. It's the Coué method. We go through the articles together, one by one. The discussion continues quietly until Saeb is interrupted by an important phone call. He leaves the meeting room. I'm left to face the Israelis alone.

Tal asks me about a change we're suggesting. Several times in the article, we refer to the 'treaty' as a whole, rather than just the 'article' on refugees. I remind him of the structure of the planned peace treaty: the article we are discussing will form an integral part of this agreement, which will also include several annexes, one of which will deal with refugees. In other words, the article is not in itself sufficient to completely resolve this issue. It is merely an agreement on the principles that should govern the settlement of the fate of Palestinian refugees. The parties will then have to agree on the technical details of implementing the solution. This is how he should understand our reference to the 'treaty' as a whole.

Tal takes me back:

'All our [Israeli] obligations regarding refugees will be included in this article. We will not discuss refugees after that. We have reached an agreement with Saeb.'

'I'm not sure I understand...' I stammer.

'This article includes all the points we will be discussing bilaterally. The Israelis will no longer be involved after that. The process will then become multilateral. That's why we want the United States to be involved. They will take the lead.'

'I thought we had agreed to first discuss the framework and principles of the refugee agreement and other permanent status issues before a new round of negotiations on the technical details...'

'No, that's not realistic. Saeb and I have agreed on this point.'

'Well, even if that is the case, it doesn't make sense. The document we are currently discussing is totally obsolete without further agreement on the details of the dossier. As it stands, all Israeli obligations would become vague commitments that could not be implemented. On the basis

Negotiations

of this document alone, how can I determine what Israel's financial contribution to refugee compensation will be? You tell us that you agree to pay a contribution, but without making any commitment as to its amount. Once again, the international community will be called upon to cover the expenses... Is that the idea? Technically, you're going to have a bilateral Israeli–Palestinian declaration of principles that will be imposed on the participants in a multilateral resolution process? Do you think they'll accept that? Have you even given it any serious thought?'

Tal becomes irritated.

'The second process could also be trilateral, with the United States,' he retorts.

'If the parties are seriously considering this option, they should start thinking about the technical, legal, and practical implications. At this stage, we should then list the clearly bilateral issues before going any further.'

Saeb comes back into the room. I immediately tell him what Tal has just told me. I urge him to tell me if we really agree with the Israelis on what they're proposing. Saeb looks away. Tal Becker cuts me off:

'Ziyad, we asked you at a previous meeting to clarify what were the legal grounds on which the Palestinians claim reparations for non-material damage."

Tal is trying to divert my attention from the trap he's set for us. Or the 'compromise'—surrender I should say, that has been previously agreed. Saeb remains silent. As if he didn't hear me. I have no choice but to hand Tal Becker a note I had prepared on the reparations due to Palestinian refugees for non-material damage suffered after sixty years of dispossession and forced exile. The discussion quickly turns to pleadings. I unroll my argument. It's mechanical, as if spoken by someone else. I know it's futile. My mind is elsewhere, stuck on the Israelis' sleight of hand, apparently validated by Saeb. Saeb quickly puts an end to the stylistic exercise:

'I know I shouldn't interrupt two lawyers in the middle of an argument but, please, let's postpone this debate.'

The meeting ends. I rush to Saeb to clarify the crucial point he is reluctant to elucidate. He has already picked up the phone. We wish him a blessed Ramadan. I stand in front of him, barely two meters away. With his hand, he beckons me not to wait. Saeb turns on his heel. He's slipping through my fingers. The file too, I get the impression, even if the knife is slow to fall. In the meantime, Habib's memory, Eissam's future, and the recognition of a part of my identity, Palestine, are still in abeyance.

X
"The Generous Offer"
September / October 2008

The peace process has stalled. As far as I can see, it's over—there's no doubt about it. Paradoxically, this not the worst-case scenario. Once again, the Palestinians were unable to reach any kind of equitable agreement with Israel.

The latest political developments in Israel have put the negotiators' last illusions to rest. Ehud Olmert is in the cross-hairs of his country's judiciary. Tzipi Livni is campaigning hard for the leadership of the Kadima party.

On the other side of the wall, Ramadan has sapped the last of the Palestinians' energy. At the end of the Muslim fast, Israelis too will take a long rest for the Jewish holidays. It's high time to move on. All that's missing is someone from Ramallah to take stock of the exit from this disastrous round of negotiations. The Palestinian house has cracks all over. In fact, the foundations had not even been laid.

After an exhausting month of August, September promises to be quieter for me. Mahmoud Abbas, Saeb Erekat, and the others are hanging on the Israeli news. It's fascinating to watch the leaders in Ramallah develop their analysis of

Israeli domestic affairs. Each has their own prognosis. Each has a favourite. What are Olmert's chances of saving his skin? Livni's chances of winning? They all seem to be passionate about it. To tell the truth, all they need is the right to vote.

On 6 September, the Israeli police put an end to the Israeli prime minister's reprieve: they recommend that Olmert be impeached for his alleged role in some murky bribery scandals. However, impeachment could take some time. Indeed, it is likely that Olmert would prefer resignation to this even more painful end. In the meantime, pending the formation of a new Israeli government coalition or the organization of new elections, he remains in office, though very weakened, it goes without saying. Livni, on the other hand, takes over the leadership of the Kadima party, turning a new page. A confrontation with Bibi Netanyahu to take over the reins of the country looms on the horizon.

And yet, amidst the Ramadan torpor, things suddenly come to a head. Surprising as it may seem, we're not quite finished with the negotiations yet. A fourth episode is about to unfold; the tragicomedy is about to resume. It's Rosh Hashanah, the Jewish New Year: Olmert has made new resolutions. In the space of a few days, while Israel and the Palestinians take their bets on the date of his resignation, he makes a series of sensational announcements. On 15 September 2008, in an interview with the newspaper *Yediot Aharonot*, Ehud Olmert stated that he had offered 98 per cent of the West Bank to the Palestinians. The same day, he expressed his sadness at the plight of the refugees. He added that Israel was 'eager to be part of an international mechanism to seek solutions to this problem.'

Just two weeks earlier, Tal Becker was arguing the opposite. Whom to believe? For Olmert, the solution to the Palestinian refugee problem must also be found within the Palestinian state, but he claims to have made a gesture in his talks with Abbas: he would have accepted that 5,000 of them return to Israel. That leaves Jerusalem. Olmert himself has so far denied that the issue is being discussed with the PLO. This does not prevent him from concluding in the press that the absence of an agreement is the result of a lack of courage on the part of his Palestinian interlocutor.

The office of the president of the Palestinian Authority, the PLO, and the NSU, are in shock. The so-called 'offer' is still a hundred leagues from what could be accepted by a 'moderate' Palestinian leader. But Olmert has finally proposed something. Not to the Palestinians, but to the media and to Israeli and international opinion. The positions put forward are indeed disconnected from what was discussed at the negotiating table. The prime minister has flouted the confidentiality agreements he had with the PLO leadership. He took his peace partners by surprise. But this former advocate of a Greater Israel, from the Jordan River to the Mediterranean, who was certainly pushed towards the exit, now asserts that he is ready for a territorial compromise. This former mayor of Jerusalem, a great promoter of the colonization of the eastern part of the city, is playing his last cards on the threshold of his political death.

He finally announced his resignation. He made a new appearance in the media, stating that Israel must withdraw from East Jerusalem and the Golan Heights. Coming from an Israeli Prime Minister, the statement is historic.

But Olmert is now only acting the part of prime minister. His time is running out. Legally, he's still in charge. But politically, he's no longer worth a shekel. The PLO, caught off guard by this sudden charity, doesn't know how to react. The spectre of the 'generous offer' of another Ehud, this time Barak, haunts the Palestinian leadership in Ramallah.[76] This time, you can't afford to miss out.

As the first voices are already being raised to assert that the Palestinians have once again missed a unique opportunity to make peace, the PLO cannot remain silent. All eyes are now on Mahmoud Abbas. Should he follow Olmert's lead? Or contradict his statements? Abbas doesn't even know the exact terms of the offer. We know no more than what is written in the newspapers. The presidency has instructed us to draft a letter to the Israeli Prime Minister's office as soon as possible: the terms of his proposal must be clarified. Our document, amply supported by our questions on each of the permanent status issues, is sent out as a matter of urgency. As far as I know, President Abbas is still awaiting a reply.

So we'll be the ones to take the fall, as usual. It's all the more galling that this time the PLO had every means of preventing such an outcome. Giving the famous letter to Condoleezza Rice would have been very good political cover. Its disclosure could have enabled us to set the record straight, to explain why negotiations with Israel

---

76. At the Camp David summit, Israeli Prime Minister Ehud Barak told the media that Yasser Arafat had refused a 'generous offer,' blaming him for the failure of the negotiations. This claim was later widely questioned by other participants at the Camp David summit. See SWISHER (Clayton E.), *The Truth About Camp David*, New York, Nation Books, 2004.

cannot succeed. Or at least cast serious doubt on Olmert's statements. The PLO made no such choice. As Saeb likes to repeat, this will just be another stab in the back. He will undoubtedly recover. Perhaps Abu Mazen will too. They've seen it all before. They're survivors. On the other hand, I wouldn't put much stock in Palestine. We've played with it enough. By dint of kicking, the ball is punctured.

My worries pile up, which has the advantage of leaving me no time to lament my fate. When I was young, I played rugby. I picked up quite a few bruises. Whenever I complained about a bad knock, my father used to tell me to get up straight away. Because the next shock always makes you forget the previous one. Palestine is a bit like that. After a while, it doesn't even hurt anymore. You don't even bother to hit back. Why bother? Palestine has been drugged by the blows for too long.

A new delaying tactic: Abu Mazen has taken us by surprise by announcing in the Israeli newspaper *Haaretz* that he is prepared to be conciliatory on the refugee issue. The article is entitled: 'We will compromise on refugees,' but the title is nevertheless misleading: it's a broken mirror of the PLO leader's words. Unfortunately, the damage is done. President Abbas has scored a fine own goal. Palestinian refugees in the territories, Lebanon, Syria, Jordan, and elsewhere will appreciate these gratuitous declarations of intent. They are made directly to the Israelis, without consulting the holders of rights that are subject to discount. And without any reciprocity.

Naturally, the article caused an uproar. The PLO chief's statement was picked up by all the Arab media. The NSU is called to the rescue. The President's office asked us to prepare language to rectify the situation. We had been trying for almost a year to arrange a meeting with him and his advisors on the subject. If only to point out to them, after almost twenty years of negotiations, that the number of refugees is not 4.5 million, as Abbas claims in *Haaretz*, but rather 7 million. I find it hard to shake off the immense feeling that it has all been a waste.

*

A new wave of panic arises a few days later. Saeb called the NSU. I wasn't the one on the other end, but I hear that is apparently agitated. The Jordanians issued him a letter on the refugee issue. They wanted to send the document to the Israeli government through diplomatic channels as soon as possible. I review the letter: the Jordanians object to any refugee agreement between the PLO and Israel being extended to Palestinians who had become Jordanian citizens. In their view, these 2 million individuals are legally represented by the Jordanian state, not the PLO. The Hashemite government is not fooled. It senses the fragility of the PLO in its negotiations with Israel and knows that the refugees are likely to pay the price. They want to secure their legal position in this respect. Amman at least had the courtesy to inform us of its intentions before forwarding its letter to the Hebrew government. I am asked to prepare a reply as soon as possible, which Saeb then forwards to the Jordanians.

Saeb Erekat got back to me two days later. The King of Jordan had instructed his Minister of Foreign Affairs to settle the dispute as soon as possible. Saeb asked me to get in touch with the minister's legal advisor to arrange a meeting. I am sent to the Jordanian capital to meet him. Alone. The aim is to convince the Jordanians that it is in their interest to continue to act in concert with the PLO in the negotiations on refugee rights. I feel like I've been sent to the front. My only weapon is a toothpick, which I'm asked to brandish like a banner.

I take a cab to the Jordanian border. Ramadan is drawing to a close. It's the last Friday of the fast. It's barely 11am but the heat is already oppressive. Traffic slows at a standstill on the outskirts of Ramallah. A dense crowd makes it impossible to approach the Qalandia *checkpoint.* Hundreds of cars sit idle. There are also buses parked in all directions. They come from all over the West Bank. Palestinians are waiting to pass the Israeli security post to be allowed to pray at the Al-Aqsa mosque. The chaos is indescribable. The area around the *checkpoint* is packed with people. The heat, the waiting, the fasting, make the situation unbearable. Motorists' spirits are fraying. Women and children are getting impatient. They scream and cry.

The Israelis have decided to close the *checkpoint.* I can hear crowds at the security post. I can make out scuffles, and I hear shots fired. It's hard to know what's going on. My driver, helped by a few Palestinians, finally manages to make his way through. Little by little, we pull away from the hustle and bustle. I keep my face glued to the window. I can't believe what has become of Palestine. This human misery is unbelievable. Many people have resigned themselves to praying, in the dust, a few steps from the *checkpoint.* A few dozen meters further on, others try to scale the wall. All in vain. Pure madness. The pilgrims will not see Jerusalem.

I arrive in Amman mid-afternoon. The Jordanian capital, empty, orderly, and soulless, is deadly quiet. The streets are deserted. Ramadan doesn't help matters. Residents are holed up in their homes. Sheltered from the heat, they wait patiently for the sun to set.

Better to stay at the hotel. I do a few laps in the pool to relax. The Jordanian advisor meets me a little later to break the fast. He's a friendly man, no more than forty. He tells me that he himself has a relative of Palestinian origin. He has been working for the Jordanian government for ten years. Before that, he studied in the United States and had also worked for the UN in New York.

I know my subject better today than I did a few months ago. I present the technical work carried out by the NSU. My message: Jordanian interests are fully compatible with the those pursued by the PLO. I also insist on our willingness to share with Jordan all information relating to our negotiations with Israel. My presentation seemed to be received well. We meet again the next day to settle the last outstanding issues. All this is constructive, even if I know that this meeting will not dispel Jordan's doubts about the PLO's current ability to achieve its goals. In short, I have the impression that they will continue to operate collectively for the time being, while remaining vigilant. The letter to the government of the Jewish state should not be sent. Yet.

Good news awaits me on my return to Ramallah: I learn that Rafic Husseini, President Abbas' advisor, has received a letter from a coalition of nearly eighty Palestinian NGOs entitled 'Refugee Rights and the Permanent Status Negotiations.'[77] This petition states that no just and lasting settlement of the Israeli–Palestinian conflict is possible without respect for the rights of refugees, foremost among which is the recognition and implementation of the right of return. The document has been signed by all Palestinian factions, including Fatah and Hamas. Quite a surprise. In times like these, it's no small feat.

On 23 September, Husseini had no choice but to organize a press conference on behalf of the president. He tried to be reassuring. While Mahmoud Abbas had argued the opposite in the Israeli press a week earlier, his chief of staff declared that no Palestinian negotiator would compromise on the sacred rights of Palestinian refugees. Sulta is drowning in contradictions. The PLO now knows what it's all about: the several million Palestinian refugees and the organizations that represent them are on their guard.

I go on vacation for a few days, with a slightly calmer mind. The risk of a bad agreement on refugees is now behind us. I feel I've helped put in place a few safeguards that will prevent the PLO from doing anything foolish in the weeks to come.

---

77. The petition submitted to the President of the Palestinian Authority is reproduced in Appendix V.

I return to Ramallah on the last day of September. Infighting has embroiled the members of the Palestinian negotiating team. Abu Alaa has distanced himself—unless he's been deliberately sidelined. I don't know what the end of the story is. The old Fatah politician has no doubt realized that he has a lot to lose by remaining involved in these dying negotiations. His recent statements on a bi-national state are probably to be seen in this context. Abbas and Saeb were less than pleased. In any case, divergent directives now circulate among the Palestinian negotiators. Some of those close to Abu Alaa obey his orders, but the majority are loyal to the President and Saeb. Such is the case of the NSU. Mahmoud Abbas was forced to clean house. The task of chairing what remains of the peace talks now falls to Saeb alone.

Unsurprisingly, the US administration exerted final pressure in an attempt to secure a joint Israeli–Palestinian document for the UN General Assembly. But to no avail. The positions were irreconcilable.

I finally have some time for myself. I'm delighted. Until now, my mind and energy have been consumed by the dark side of Palestine. On 17 October 2008, I attended the national soccer team's first official match on Palestinian territory. In Ram[78] just a few kilometres from Jerusalem, with the wall as a backdrop, Palestine took on Jordan. Some of the players on the Palestinian team, originally from Chile, do not speak

---

78. See map p. 94.

Arabic. The few Gazans on the team only arrived *by extreme effort* for the match. They didn't even have a chance to train with the rest of their partners. On the Jordanian side, more than half the players are of Palestinian origin.

The stadium is packed. Tickets are checked by Fatah supporters on an individual basis. It's a joyous chaos. Palestinians are perched on the stadium floodlights. In the absence of folding seats, they will follow the match from up there. The Palestinian anthem rings out: *Baladi, baladi*, 'my country, my country.' The stadium, the people of Palestine, erupts with emotion. I get goose bumps.

The Palestinian identity seems more alive than ever. At the Al-Kasaba theatre, Ramallah's cultural centre, I attend the premiere of the film *Salt of the Sea*, a Franco-Palestinian co-production. The film deals with the actuality of the right to return. Due to the lack of a visa from Israel, the director was unable to attend this first screening in Palestine. The film will have its small success in France.

More than ever, Palestine culture is expressing itself through culture and sport. The contrast with the decay of Palestinian political representation in the territories and Israel is immense. Palestinians continue to be denied recognition of their most basic rights by the state that presides over their destiny, Israel. Politically, the Palestinians are clinically dead.

Even the Palestinian dead are not accorded the respect they are due: I know today what it's like with the abandoned graves, lost in the public garden next to the American consulate in West Jerusalem. The garden is called Independence Park; the cemetery is Palestinian. For a few shekels in the parking meter, my car can park here, at the foot of these steles. On the other hand, Palestinians of the Muslim faith whose forebears are buried here have not been allowed access to these graves for decades.

This is not the end of the story: at the end of October 2008, the Israeli Supreme Court put an end to a long dispute over the fate of these tombs. The Israeli court has just agreed that a 'museum of tolerance' should be built on the remains of the Muslim cemetery. Its purpose will be to promote coexistence between Jews, Christians, and Muslims in the Holy City. So be it. Work resumed without delay. The Simon Wiesenthal Project, a Jewish organization based in Los Angeles, is behind the effort. They aim to create a conference centre, theatre, and adult and children's museums covering Jewish history and Israel's relations with its Arab neighbours.

The decision of the highest court in the 'only democracy in the Middle East' is naturally well-founded: no objections were raised in 1960 when the fledgling Israeli municipality of Jerusalem (which at the time extended only to the west of the city) decided to build a parking lot on a small part of the cemetery. There is therefore no legitimate reason today to block the construction of the museum, planned for the entire site. The Israeli court simply enjoined the management of the beautiful project to reach an agreement with the Israel Antiquities Authority to either relocate the bodies for their final transfer or install a barrier between the ground and the foundations of the new building to prevent damage to the tombs.

A new 'generous offer,' I presume.

XI

OBAMA

NOVEMBER / DECEMBER 2008

When I wake up on 4 November, the forty-fourth president of the United States of America is Black. Barack (Hussein) Obama has been elected to the White House. A dream has come true. America went to bed in the early hours of the morning after a night of collective hysteria. The rest of the world woke up with stars in their eyes. All eyes are on him.

Poor guy.

This new hope, this rejuvenating breath, offers me nothing. I get out of bed with a heavy body, weighed down by too much Palestine. For some time now, I've been getting up every day with no energy and an empty mind. It's been many long weeks since I had any hope. This historic occasion could at least have served as a diversion. I didn't even bother to turn on the TV. Amorphous, I just go about my business. The illusion of movement is the only thing that can save me from the fall.

At NSU, many people arrive late that morning. This was due to the long vigil dedicated to the American election. We're not fully staffed until late morning. We barely have time to talk about the new political situation before we're caught up in another news item, our own. It takes us by surprise.

More and more phone calls are coming in from East Jerusalem. Before long, our switchboard is ringing off the hook. We receive reports of a large number of Israeli soldiers, police and bulldozers in the Al-Bustan neighbourhood.[79] Around a hundred houses are threatened with immediate destruction. The inhabitants, evicted from their homes, call for help. Earlier in the morning, five houses were razed to the ground in the Shu 'fat and Beit Hanina neighbourhoods,[80] also in the eastern part of Jerusalem.

Two of our colleagues are quickly on the scene. Scuffles broke out between Palestinians displaced from their homes and the Israeli army, which responded to the disorder with live ammunition and tear gas. European and American diplomats have also reached the scene of these events. They can only helplessly survey the damage. The Israeli municipality, whose sphere of action illegally extends into East Jerusalem, is reportedly planning to create a municipal park on the site of the houses it is in the process of demolishing. The garden is to be called David's Park.

None of the PLO dignitaries were present at the scene. We managed to contact them in the early afternoon. They claim not to know anything about it. One of them is reassuring, promising to report the events to President Abu Mazen for inclusion in the next Quartet meeting in Sharm El Sheikh. The officials dodge us all afternoon.

---

79. See map p. 94.
80. See map p. 94.

The truth is that PLO representatives do not wish to visit the site. More than a confrontation with the Israelis, they fear a face-to-face meeting with their own people. In Jerusalem's Palestinian neighbourhoods, the criticism is as much about the Authority's inaction as it is about Israeli action. Some even believe that the destruction being carried out today is simply the result of negotiations between the two parties: the neighbourhoods being demolished are those which the PLO has agreed to cede to the Israelis.

After a few hours, we have a clearer picture. Israel is taking advantage of Obama's election day to carry out a massive house demolition campaign in East Jerusalem. And that's not all: Israel chose the same day, 4 November 2008, to carry out new incursions into Gaza. With general indifference, the Israeli government violated the ceasefire agreement they made with Hamas a scant few months ago. The result: six Hamas militants killed and a Gaza Strip once again on the brink, with Islamists promising to retaliate to avenge their dead.

The timing of these operations is so crude that no one at NSU even bothers to comment on it. The world is without security. Israeli violence escalates, without safeguards. The American guardian was nothing more than a scarecrow who could no longer fool aggressors.[81] But it's even worse without him.

---

81. From the Annapolis conference to the day of the demolitions, Israel destroyed 94 Palestinian homes in East Jerusalem. During the same period, a further 235 Palestinian homes and other structures were demolished in the rest of the West Bank.

Obama

In Washington, as the presidential transition period gets underway, Bush and Obama are playing the same score. That of silence. It wasn't until the following day, the 5th, that news came from Obama's side: the future president had offered the post of chief of staff to a certain Rahm Emmanuel. A native of Chicago, he is said to be a well-informed and feared politician in the Democratic Party: a man of the establishment with a strong character. He's also a very religious man, the son of an Irgun member who volunteered to serve in the Israeli army during the first Gulf War in 1991. His war-mongering stance even earned him the nickname 'Rahm Bo.' Let's be honest: it's not very reassuring. But let's be fair: the man must be judged by his actions.

This must also apply to Obama.

The following day, an interview with Rahm Emmanuel's father appeared in the Israeli newspaper *Maa'riv*. Asked whether his son would defend the interests of the Jewish state in the White House, the Israeli replied: 'Of course my son will influence the president to become pro-Israel. You think my son is an Arab? He's not going there to clean the White House floors. He's going there to do serious work.'

In the space of a single day, the Israeli government and Rahm Emmanuel's father have deprived the Palestinians of a new right: the right to hope for a better world from Obama.

*

So much has already been said and written about Obama. In a Middle East torn asunder, his background, his face and his name are all intriguing. "Abu Hussein", as he's been somewhat hastily renamed around here, could be one of us, or at any rate more capable of understanding the aspirations of Arabs, Muslims and Palestinians than Bush.

Personally, I'm all the more sympathetic to Barack Obama because I've always dreamed of being African American. No kidding. A failed six-foot-five basketball player, I'm a pure product of my generation. Awakened to the world of music and entertainment by Michael Jackson, I then grew up in contact with the demanding sounds of rap. I was drawn to the hard-hitting cinema of Spike Lee and fascinated by the spectacle and excess of NBA basketball stars. My friends and I identified with the Black struggle in the United States. Obama's arrival on the American scene cannot leave me indifferent.

The Palestinian in me sees things differently. At the end of July 2008, in Sderot, a frequent target of Hamas rocket fire, Obama asserted that the Israelis had the right to retaliate against attacks from Gaza. He had not a word to say about the terrible plight of the Gazans and the blockade they suffer. Israelis, led by Ehud Barak, were quick to interpret these statements as a carte blanche from the presidential election favourite. In front of the American Jewish organization AIPAC,[82] Obama went even further: he affirmed that Jerusalem is 'the one, indivisible and eternal capital of Israel.'[83] This leaves little room for doubt: the new

---

82. AIPAC (American Israeli Public Affairs Committee) is a lobbying organization promoting Israeli interests and policies in the United States. It is particularly active and influential with the US Congress and the executive branch.
83. Faced with the uproar caused by this statement, Barack Obama later retracted it.

American president remains and will remain dependent on his voters and campaign supporters. The incursions into Gaza and Israel's policy of ethnic cleansing of East Jerusalem will continue.

Of course, in the final days of the presidential race, we learned that Obama had a 'Palestinian friend': Columbia University professor Rashid Khalidi. This suspicious acquaintance was the subject of one of the latest arrows launched by Republican candidate John McCain's running mate, Sarah Palin, in an attempt to destabilize the Illinois senator. Fox News and CNN seized on the subject, saying anything and everything about the professor, but to no avail. History had already chosen its side.

Without wishing to deny Obama's sensitivity to the Palestinian problem—which his predecessor clearly lacked—I do not believe he is capable of substantially changing the American position on the Israeli–Palestinian conflict. The United States will remain Israel's most important ally, and the American president's room for manoeuvre on this issue will remain extremely limited. Obama's oratory skills, his charisma, and his mixed-race identity even present a major risk: the new American head of state is creating inordinate expectations. These expectations are likely to be matched by disillusionment.

To be honest, I haven't expected much from the United States for a long time now. I've come to believe these US-sponsored negotiations to be a waste of time. Worse still, the pseudo-peace talks have already cost us too much in human and political capital. The upcoming transition in the United States will be another opportunity for Israel to clean up its act in the territories and continue to advance on the ground. I also know now that the PLO is not in a position to obtain an equitable agreement from Israel. Make no mistake, this has never been the case in the past. And I seriously doubt it will be so in the future.

So I decided to face the obvious. I decided not to renew my contract with NSU when it expires on 15 January 2009. This is an opportunity for me to take stock of my year in Palestine On 9 November, I notified my employer of my resignation and the reasons for it in a letter:

'You may recall that my decision to join NSU a year ago was not an easy one. Initially, I had come here to teach [...] So, despite a keen interest in the position offered by NSU, I was slow to accept it. I was ready to make a technical contribution to the development of the refugee dossier, which was already well advanced. I was happy to be put in a position to promote the NSU's work. However, in view of the political reservations and fears of which you are already aware, I was also sceptical about the Annapolis process. I finally made up my mind and decided to join the NSU, and to commit myself fully to it, believing that this effort was perhaps the last chance for negotiations to lead to "the two-state solution."

In November 2007, the objective was clearly set: the creation of a Palestinian state by the end of 2008. One year after the Annapolis summit, the result is as follows:

Nearly 500 Palestinians were killed and just under 2,000 wounded by Israeli forces.

Israel has dramatically accelerated its colonization efforts in the West Bank, including East Jerusalem. Of the

Obama

hundreds of *checkpoints* and other physical barriers to the free movement of Palestinians within the occupied territories, not a single obstacle has been removed.

The country is still divided, and the PLO continues to pursue an illusory peace settlement with Israel, rather than national reconciliation.

What I have described above is naturally not the responsibility of the NSU, whose mandate is to prepare and provide technical support for the negotiations. However, it is my responsibility to decide whether I wish to continue to be personally involved, in view of the events of the past year and the expected direction of the PLO. At this stage, I am convinced that it is not in the Palestinians' interest to see this process continue. I therefore no longer wish to be associated with it.

I must add that the refugee situation is particularly catastrophic. A commonly held view among refugees, Palestinians and Arab parties is that the PLO no longer represents the views and interests of most Palestinians. The PLO now seems inclined to use the historic rights of the Palestinian refugees, which remain at the heart of the conflict, as a bargaining chip in the ongoing talks, which is a disastrous political gamble. I'm sure you'll understand that I have my own red lines, since the refugee problem remains a deeply personal issue for me and my family [...].'

The NSU manager tries to convince me to stay. Clumsily, he offers me a big raise to keep me going. This offer makes me even more nervous. Failing to convince me, he at least asks me to wait a little before informing the PLO of my decision. According to him, the situation could improve in the near future, particularly on the front of internal Palestinian reconciliation. I'm far from convinced. But I agree to follow his instructions. I won't inform Erekat and Areikat for the time being. I'll continue to act 'as if' for another two months.

The Israelis don't pretend. In East Jerusalem, the destruction of homes multiplies. In the early hours of 9 November, they evicted a Palestinian family, the Al Kurds, from their home in Sheikh Jarrah.[84]

The Al Kurd family had lived in this house since 1956. At that time, Jordan and UNRWA had set up housing to accommodate Palestinian refugee families waiting to return to their homes in Jaffa,[85] Ramle, and West Jerusalem, all of which are now in Israel. The family was forced to become residents of East Jerusalem, after being expelled by Jewish militias from their homes in Talpiot[86] (now West Jerusalem) and Jaffa in 1948. Since 1967, the Al Kurds have been under threat from settler organizations. The settlers have forcibly occupied part of the premises since 2001. Despite a complaint lodged by the US State Department last July challenging the Al Kurds' expulsion, the settlers are about to see their relentless efforts pay off. This land, East Jerusalem, is becoming theirs.

Sixty years after the Nakba, the Al Kurd family have been tossed back on the streets, with nowhere to go. God knows what the future holds for them. In the meantime, they're

---

84. See map p. 94.
85. See maps p. 8.
86. See map p. 94.

Obama

not giving up. With the help of their neighbours and a few activists, the Al Kurd family is going to pitch a tent in front of their house. Twenty-six other Palestinian homes in the same neighbourhood are under direct Israeli threat. More than 500 people are affected.

This 9 November closes with a statement from the Quartet. I glanced at it out of curiosity, with the slightly feigned detachment of the young resigning member that I am: no mention of the situation in East Jerusalem, no word on Gaza. On the other hand, we learn that Mahmoud Abbas and Tzipi Livni have reached agreements on the principles that should govern the negotiation process—almost a year after it began. Essentially, they agreed on the need to continue direct and uninterrupted negotiations and the principle that nothing can be considered decided until full agreement has been reached on all permanent status issues.

The Quartet welcomes this progress. The Quartet has blinkers on. It refuses to see in these negotiations the trompe-l'œil that masks Israel's aggressive, land-grabbing policies in Palestinian territory. To make matters worse, the Quartet seems to have amnesia. The Israeli–Palestinian declaration is virtually identical to the one issued in Annapolis in November 2008.

*

The following days confirmed my decision to resign. It's irrevocable. I'm no help to anyone in my position. I don't have the means to fight. I'm just another decoy, lost in the smokescreen of the 'peace process.' I know that the current balance of power makes any search for compromise with the Israelis illusory. In the future, perhaps. But with another objective for negotiation: there is no longer enough land or water[87] to create a sovereign and independent State of Palestine, free from any Israeli presence.

Nobody could convince me to stay. No one close to me or at the NSU could find the arguments. Quite the opposite. To be fair, only two people were able to question my decision, for a few hours at least. They were Mohammed and Ingrid, my contacts at Badil, a Bethlehem-based organization that defends and promotes the rights of refugees. Their opinion, based on a decade of exceptional work in the field, was important to me. Their words resonated strongly: at present, no institution on the Palestinian side can be trusted. The Palestinian cause survives thanks to trustworthy individuals. In their eyes, my presence within the NSU was an asset. They believe that we can hold out for a few more years, and that the future may not be as bleak

---

87. The problem of water, often neglected by commentators on Israeli–Palestinian news, is one of the permanent status issues that also awaits resolution. Since the occupation of the Palestinian territories began in 1967, Israel has taken control of almost all Palestinian waters and denied Palestinians the right to access and exploit their own resources. Today, Israel appropriates 89 per cent of available shared water resources, leaving the rest to the Palestinians. The average Palestinian receives 60 litres of water per day for domestic use, with some communities having to make do with less than 10 litres per day (particularly in Gaza). This is well below the minimum daily consumption of 100 litres recommended by the World Health Organization. The average individual daily consumption in Israel is 280 litres, more than four times that in the occupied territories.

as it seems. The parameters of the fight are gradually being redrawn. I hope they're right.

Mohammed gazed at me with his clear eyes, a benevolent smile at the corner of his lips. He told me about his first steps in promoting refugee rights on Nakba Day. He was alone, or almost alone, at the Damascus Gate in East Jerusalem. Often, he was met with indifference or amused contempt by many Palestinians. Just as frequently, he was spat at and insulted by Israeli passers-by. He told me this in a calm, gentle tone, without any bitterness, as if driven by an unshakeable faith in justice. Only a few years have passed, and the world now knows that Israel's birthday is also that of the Palestinian Nakba. For the time of this meeting, I feel like an idiot, me and my moods, before the saintliness of Mohammed and Ingrid. Palestine survives thanks to them and all those who give their lives to this cause with the utmost dignity. I have decided to leave the NSU. It is likely that I will leave Palestine sometime in 2009. But I vow to find the best way to make myself useful in the future.

*

Each NSU councillor has been asked to work with his committee leader to prepare an update on negotiations on each of the permanent status dossiers. I prepare for the refugees on my own and get an appointment with Saeb to take stock. I go to his office on Thursday, 13 November, just before a meeting with all the Palestinian negotiators.

In my opinion, the way the refugee negotiations were conducted was catastrophic. We narrowly avoided disaster. The truth is, we were saved by circumstances totally outside our control. In no particular order, and the list is not exhaustive: we couldn't find a negotiator; coordination with President Abbas was woefully inadequate—as was the coordination we should have ensured with the Arab countries where the refugees reside, who are stakeholders in this issue, as well. I'm also convinced that we should have reported back to the refugee organizations, one way or another, on the progress of the talks. The PLO cannot continue to negotiate the individual rights of Palestinian refugees behind their backs.

I realize that it's actually a very heavy balance sheet that I will present to the chief Palestinian negotiator. I come to him with the aim of presenting things in a positive light and proposing improvements that seem appropriate. I can't risk alienating him. I can't afford to lose his ear right at the start of the meeting:

'First of all, Doctor, I think it's important to remember the enormous pressure that the Americans and Israelis exerted on this issue, particularly over the summer. The Israelis wanted to impose American leadership on us. Rice was determined to get us to back off on the refugee issue. Even the Jordanians at one point seemed inclined to play their cards alone, independently of our negotiations with Israel. On all these fronts, when we couldn't find a negotiator to take charge of the dossier, we held firm...'

Saeb cuts me off:

'Ziyad, really, I'm very happy with the way I negotiated the dossier. I think we worked skilfully, and I intend to continue to do so.'

His reaction takes me by surprise. Saeb tells me this with such aplomb—he looks proud of himself. I try to remind him of his initial reservations about the case.

'Of course, Doctor, but perhaps now that all this has calmed down, we could take the time to look for a negotiator who would like to be briefed and could take over our work?'

'No, no, no, no, no. I know the file now. We've done a great job. In fact, I'm going to suggest to Abu Mazen that he give me full responsibility for the file to avoid any coordination problems with the President's office.'

As surprised as ever, I continue to review my list of prescriptions:

'Doctor, now that negotiations have broken down, perhaps it's time to return to civilian organizations to discuss the refugee issue, at least informally. Doctor, you need to know that there is a real expectation on their part. People are worried. I thought we could organize a small meeting, with four or five representatives of refugee NGOs, to take the pulse of the camps, and pass on any information we feel we should—'

'No, no,' Saeb, again, cuts me off curtly. 'I don't want the NGOs or any other third party on my back. I don't want anyone interfering with the way I negotiate the dossier.'

He punctuates his warning with a knowing look. I pretend to take note of his answer and continue:

'Doctor, what about coordination with the host states?[88] We've done a good job of preserving the link with Jordan, but I

----

88. States where most Palestinian refugees live: Jordan, Syria, Lebanon.

believe that coordination with Syria and Lebanon, on a similar flexible and confidential basis, is also necessary to ensure the future implementation of any agreement in these countries.'

'No, no, that's not an option. I said no third-party interference.'

A knock at the office door. We're told it's time to go to the meeting with the other Palestinian negotiators. Saeb Erekat stands up, and I have to follow him. End of conversation.

*

The PLO seems equally overwhelmed by the deteriorating situation in East Jerusalem. In fact, everything is linked. Yesterday's refugees from Jaffa, West Jerusalem, and elsewhere are today's residents of East Jerusalem. Perhaps tomorrow they will become residents of Ramallah. And the day after tomorrow? Jordan? Who knows.

In the space of just a few days, the Israelis have erected a barrier around the Al Kurd family and the residents of Sheikh Jarrah who refuse to leave the site confiscated by the army. The Al Kurd family's tent has already been dismantled and reassembled several times under the threat of bulldozers. The Israeli municipality is adamant: a parking lot is to be built on the site of the Al Kurds' home. The project has the backing of Livni's cabinet. But the Al Kurds are not letting their guard down. Their struggle has become a symbol of the Palestinians' fight for their land.

On 23 November Mohammed Al Kurd, the head of the family, died of long-standing diabetes aggravated by heart problems. His condition had worsened since he was evicted from his home on 9 November. He left his wife, Oum Kamal, in sole charge of the future of his five children and the rest of the family.

Whether it's 1948 or 2008, the Nakba continues. The memory of my grandfather is not far away. I still don't know what to make of it, but I know today that it will never leave me.

On 3 December, Oum Kamal Al Kurd made the news. She has decided to take her future into her own hands. The time has come for her to exercise her right to return to her home in West Jerusalem. A non-violent demonstration organized with the help of NGOs and civil society activists was stopped on the outskirts of her home. She had to turn back. No doubt she'll be back. If not her, then someone else.

Once again, the PLO was overwhelmed by the events. Its people are no longer waiting for it. Palestine has been leaderless for some time now—four years, to be precise.

The 9th of December 2008 marks the fourth anniversary of Arafat's death. Fatah organizes a rally in Ramallah, a stone's throw from the NSU. I watch it on TV. Buoyed by the clamour and bravos of the crowd, Saeb Erekat is filmed dancing the *dabke*[89] amidst a crowd of enthusiastic Palestinians. I can't believe my eyes. What's wrong with him? How can he justify this behaviour when we're commemorating Arafat's death? It seems to be his way of exorcising the great Palestinian shipwreck. As an affront to destiny, like Zorba, he laughs out loud at his failure.

---

89. The *dabke is* a traditional dance popular in Palestine and Lebanon.

Saeb, against all odds, has chosen life—the choice of life under occupation. Doesn't he usually tell his foreign interlocutors that his worst failure would be to see one of his children become a terrorist one day? That, or to see them leave the country. Saeb lives in Palestine. Maybe I'm just passing through. Hamas won't forgive him his dance. The chief negotiator, the PLO's 'collaborator,' was snapped up the very next day by the Islamists, who denounced these demonstrations of joy unworthy of the raïs' memory.[90]

*

The Israeli and Palestinian delegations agreed to hold a final debriefing meeting on each issue. The aim is to take stock of the progress made after a year of talks. We are just a few days away from the end of 2008. The play has been awaiting its Act V for weeks now.

For this last session on refugees, the two delegations are larger. Saeb Erekat and I are accompanied by the NSU coordinator. On the Israeli side, Tal Becker is accompanied by Udi Dekel, the head of their delegation, and two other advisors. Among them is an Israeli Arab. Saeb embraces him warmly and calls out to him in Palestinian dialect on his arrival.

It's 11 o'clock in the morning, and we have an hour. The discussion turns to lengthy considerations of the current political situation. Livni suggested in a recent interview that the future of Israeli Arabs lay in the future Palestinian state. Saeb expands on the dramatic significance of this

---

90. President", in Arabic.

statement. Finally, Udi Dekel asks him to report on the progress of the refugee talks.

I've prepared Saeb. All eyes turn to the chief Palestinian negotiator. But only a few words come out of his mouth:

'Tal will report on our work.'

I suddenly tense up. It's Tal Becker, the Israeli, Livni's chief of staff, who's going to take stock of the talks on Palestinian refugees. His notes are ready:

'The way the discussions on refugees were conducted was discreet and serious. We avoided unnecessary pressure. We moved forward methodically, point by point. I think these refugee negotiations can serve as a model: we started discussing the issue as early as February. I think it was useful for Saeb and me to have these long exchanges before putting anything down on paper. It was only after these discussions that the exchange of proposals began between the two parties.'

I look at Saeb. He's off. Absent. Tal Becker finishes his report. All eyes turn back to Saeb. He finally articulates a few sentences:

'I completely agree with Tal. The final decisions will rest with our leaders. Ehud Olmert and Abu Mazen discussed the question of return. I think we worked constructively. The refugee issue is part of a package and is linked to the resolution of other issues. We agree on the text. Everything will make sense once we have a definitive idea of the package.'

Saeb's Israeli interlocutors nod knowingly. I'm living a nightmare. Right from the start, the dice were loaded. Saeb concludes:

'As far as I'm concerned, that's fine. Unless anyone has any questions or anything to add, I think we can move on.'

The NSU coordinator has a question. Then I take the floor. There's so much to say, I don't know where to start. I do my best to get to the point: the level of detail in the article is insufficient, it doesn't include a definition of the notion of refugees, no clear commitment on Israel's financial contribution... The truth is, I'm fed up. It's unmistakeable. I'm feverish too. They're all staring at me with their round eyes. I feel like they think I'm an alien.

Tal cites the 'deal' with Saeb:

'As I said, we discussed these issues with Saeb back in February: we agree that a balance needs to be struck on the level of detail the refugee article should include.'

Udi Dekel concludes the discussion:

'Thank you. I think the article reflects your discussions. This is probably the best way to proceed: isolate the political decisions that will have to be made by our leaders. This article should be considered as the one that will appear in the agreement. The mechanism will be responsible for its implementation. If we identify other needs, we can always agree on subsequent arrangements.'

The meeting's over. The meeting lasted just over half an hour. Thirty minutes is the time allotted to the 7 million refugees today. The next hour will be devoted to the fate of the 11,000 Palestinian prisoners. I pass. Saeb thanks me for my help. I say goodbye to the Israelis.

I leave the room, outraged. The Israeli delegation's legal advisor follows me out and asks why I'm so upset. Her attention seems sincere. I tell her everything's fine. I don't doubt for a moment that she doesn't believe a word of it. The NSU coordinator also leaves the meeting:

'Ziyad, don't worry, you can sort it all out. You've done it before, you can make up for it!'

I think she's serious. My words are lost in the void:

'Of course not. There's nothing I can do about it now. It's a disaster. It's a disaster...'

XII

GAZA,

THE PUNISHMENT
DECEMBER 2008 / JANUARY 2009

I landed on American soil on 26 December 2008. On the 27th, the Israelis bombed the Gaza Strip. I knew nothing about it. I swear, I didn't.

I had decided to go on vacation a few weeks earlier with some friends to celebrate the New Year in the American West. It was going to be a major cultural experience for me. We had put San Diego, the Grand Canyon, and Las Vegas on the agenda. Not Gaza. It was Karim, my journalist friend, also on the trip, who heard the news on TV. CNN and Fox News spared no American motel. Tsahal's Operation Cast Lead had no trouble finding us here.

The two major US networks are devoting non-stop *live coverage* to the Israeli operations. Karim is already looking on the Internet for a plane ticket to go back. I don't know what I'm doing here. I imagine the F-16s Saeb was talking about punishing the people of Gaza.

These are not the images that scroll over and over on the small screen. American journalists are reporting from

Sderot. This Israeli town near Gaza is under direct threat from Hamas rocket fire. On the screen, the reporter is always helmeted, wearing a bulletproof vest. His gaze betrays the fear of taking a missile to the head. We share his anguish. Like that of the Israeli children taken to shelters. And that of their parents, who testify, worried but relieved to see the army finally taking things in hand.

The Israeli General Staff distils its communications in a scientific manner. The discourse is honed. The work of a wordsmith. Justification for armed operations: Hamas has broken the ceasefire. Their war aims: putting an end to rocket attacks on southern Israel. Respect for international law: the Israeli military pays the utmost attention to protecting civilians. Gazans are even informed in advance of bombardments. Tsahal spokesmen tell us this tirelessly every day, affably, in perfect English.

America's wide-open spaces unfold before our eyes, along Route 66. The media circus continues. We are caught up in the news. The contrast between the images on the screen and the human toll on the Palestinian side is growing daily. An abyss. Since the start of the bombardments, the Israelis have completely closed off the Gaza Strip to the media. It's hard to know what's really going on. But we can't believe what we're being sold.

After a few days, the American media are finally moving away from sensationalism and asking the right questions: who really violated the ceasefire between Hamas and Israel? What are the losses and destruction on the Gaza side? Isn't Hamas the elected representative of the Palestinian people in the 2006 elections?

CNN has found a French expert to answer all these questions. And to reassure us. Bernard-Henri Lévy, "BHL", *the French philosopher,* has been in the media since the first days of the bombings. There's no escaping it, even in the United States. Images from Al Jazeera begin to give an idea of the scale of the disaster on the Palestinian side. But BHL, in his sexy white shirt and sexy Franglais, has an answer for everything. If casualties are mounting in Gaza, it's because Hamas is using the civilian population as a *human shield.* Was Hamas democratically elected? 'Yes, but remember,' asserts the Saint-Germain-des-Prés philosopher, 'Hitler also came to power through the ballot box.' The argument hits the nail on the head. The CNN journalist is spellbound.

The Grand Canyon is under snow. It's a fairy tale. In Gaza, too, it's freezing cold. I received a message from a Palestinian friend: he and his neighbours have had to break their windows to avoid shards of glass caused by Israeli bombs. They are holed up in their homes. Humanitarian aid is blocked. Water and electricity are in short supply.

The scenery in Arizona is grandiose. We stop at an Indian reservation we almost didn't notice. A lone, poorly main-tained sign indicates the entrance to an area we vaguely understand to be self-governed. Forgotten. There are only a few natives here. With their weathered complexions and sad smiles, they are the descendants of one of history's great genocides. Behind their stalls, they sell jewellery and other trinkets. It's like Bethlehem before Christmas. The wall, which cuts the city in two, is killing life there. What's left is a little handicraft. Folklore for the Christian pilgrims

Gaza, the Punishment

who still stop here. I want to take a souvenir back to Saeb. I hesitate between a peace pipe or a bow and arrow. It makes my friends smile.

We reach Las Vegas. Gaza is already off the front pages. Palestine isn't on anyone's radar screen here. We're in the city of vice, Sin City. A cab driver, a Republican, a little reactive but sympathetic, explains to us why he has finally decided to vote for Obama. He wishes us a good time and says, *"Whatever happens in Vegas, stays in Vegas."*

On the plasma screen of the palatial suite where we've made our home, the victims continue to fall in Gaza. CNN doesn't linger. I flick to basketball. I wander like a zombie through the casino. I'm handed flyers featuring Vegas strippers. I'm thinking about starting a collection. My friends are playing poker. I skim the roulette tables, alone.

We're still going to try to celebrate the New Year in style. We've decided to spend the evening in Old Town Las Vegas. An American-style show is on the program. We're in the street with hundreds of other onlookers. Many are already seriously drunk. The highlights of the year flash by in a grand sound-and-light show projected onto the street. Then comes the traditional countdown: "10, 9, 8, 7, 6, 5, 4, 3, 2, 1... 0!" A clamour erupts from the crowd: 2009, that's it, we're there!

The year 2009 arrives with still no Palestinian state.

I embrace my friends. I smile. Though maybe it's a grimace. My silence immediately catches up with me. I blame myself for not enjoying the evening. Shortly afterwards, I turn my back on my gang.

I play the casino of a chic hotel on the Strip.[91] I take a seat at the table with a dubious-looking Russian and an Italian flanked by a buxom woman. My partners tonight reek of dishonesty, but they're big players. I'm at the end of my stay. After a few warm-up games in the previous days, I feel like I'm finally in the big leagues. I decide to bet everything I have left at this table. It's now or never.

The game starts badly. My numbers aren't coming out.

A third man, a drunken Englishman, approaches us. His presence soon becomes a burden. Positioned just behind my shoulder, he takes me to task in a cavernous voice:

'It's bad for you, my friend, it's bad for you...'

I try to ignore it and persist in playing the same numbers as usual. One by one, my chips slip through my fingers. The Englishman starts to insult me:

'*Fuck man*, you're getting fleeced, go home, go home to bed. You don't belong here!'

Security immediately intervenes and forces him to leave the table. He has no place in our small, permitted circle. The dealer gives me a friendly nod, as if to reassure me. I'm under the game master's protection. Changing strategy is out of the question. My luck's bound to change. In just over an hour, I've lost almost my entire stake—over $2,000. I have one last chip left. I give it to the American dealer who caused my loss and wish him a Happy New Year. He replies, politely, with a smile that is meant to be comforting: '*Thank you, sir. Happy New Year.*'

---

91. The Strip is the main thoroughfare through Las Vegas, where the most excessive and extravagant hotels follow one another.

I leave the casino with empty pockets. I feel a huge weight has been lifted. The year 2008, the year of Annapolis and the PLO's abortive gamble, is behind me.

*

I return to Paris on 3 January 2009 on my sister's birthday. The IDF launches its ground offensive on the same day. I'm surprised by the scale of the initiative, but perhaps the worst is yet to come: the Israelis have a free hand until 20 January, the date of Barack Obama's inauguration as President of the United States. Until then, they will no doubt continue to take advantage of the international leadership vacuum.

I'm not due to return to Ramallah until 10 January. I have contacted the Palestine delegation in France to make myself available to them. They are overwhelmed, harassed by the media, who are compounding their coverage of the situation in Gaza. Solicited by the Quai d'Orsay, which is busy on the diplomatic front. Palestinian representation in France is paralyzed by Sulta's ambiguous stance on events. After condemning the Israeli attacks, Abbas was quick to blame Hamas for the invasion. Quickly, he finds himself under fire from the whole of Palestinian and Arab opinion.

From NSU, it's radio silence. I call to find out what's going on. I'm told that the project has been short-circuited. The political situation is deemed too sensitive by the Authority, which wants to handle the situation on its own. My colleagues, powerless as they are, see, as I do, the damage and the daily toll of civilian casualties. In Ramallah, demonstrations in support of the people of Gaza were violently repressed by the Palestinian security forces. Demonstrators, including women, are beaten, and some were imprisoned.

Mahmoud Abbas's mandate as head of the Palestinian Authority expired on 9 January. The event goes completely unnoticed. The same day, I inform my employer of my intention to stay in Paris. My contract with NSU runs until the 15th of this month. But I've decided not to return to Ramallah until I feel more useful there than here. There's no way I'm going back if it's to witness Abu Mazen's deafening silences. If it's to witness the repression of Palestinian civilians guilty of publicly demonstrating their solidarity with Gaza.

I find myself alone in Paris. With no mandate, no label, I'm ready to do what's needed. I'm sent to the set of '*Le Ring*,' a debate hosted by Michel Field on LCI. I arrive at the studio early. I'm dressed in my best suit. Clean-shaven, I look like a young movie star. Palestine has never looked so inoffensive. I meet the other guests. I'm not sure how to introduce myself to them. I try, 'Hello, Ziyad Clot, lawyer, nice to meet you.' Obviously, that's not enough. The first person I shake hands with, a fellow lawyer, gives me a furtive glance. He doesn't linger and heads off to the make-up room. The second, a representative of a French Jewish community organization, tanned, stout and Arab-looking, frowns. I feel compelled to add something: 'I'm French of Palestinian origin.' He stares at me. He glares at me, then casually asks, 'Are you a Muslim?'

Throughout the debate, he barked: 'Israel has no moral lessons to learn from anyone, sir! Israel has no moral lessons to learn from anyone!'

A few days later, it's France 24's turn, in English then in French. My opponent, an Israeli historian and journalist, is much more courteous. We hit it off before the debate. We have a mutual friend. I begin the program by listing the names of entire families decimated by the Gaza expedition. Later in the debate, I point out that the legal characterization of Israeli military operations remains to be determined. I assert that 'certain elements are akin to quasi-genocide.' The Israeli snaps. It may have been clumsy. But was it excessive?

I'll go back to my law books a little later. Article II of the Convention on the Prevention and Punishment of the Crime of Genocide defines genocide 'as one of the following acts committed with intent to destroy, in whole or in part, a national, ethnical, racial or religious group, as such:
- murder of group members
- serious harm to the physical or mental integrity of group members
- intentional subjection of the group to conditions of existence intended to bring about its total or partial physical destruction [...].'

You be the judge.

I'm exhausted. I can't sleep. I'm overwhelmed with emotion. One evening—or morning, I don't know—I broke down crying.

French public opinion is itself shaken. The violence of the images broke certain taboos. Tongues are loosening. Parallels are drawn. Gaza is described by some as the Palestinians' Warsaw ghetto. The worsening situation in the Middle East has led to fears of a resurgence of communal violence in France. As a Frenchman, I'm worried about the tensions created here by the punishment inflicted on Gaza. As a privileged witness to the Palestinian tragedy, it would be criminal to remain silent.

A rally in support of the Palestinians is being organized in Paris on 10 January. I'm not accustomed to these collective actions in support of 'the cause.' But there's no doubt in my mind today: my place is in this procession with all those who, like me, are appalled by what's happening in Gaza. I joined the march with a few friends. For most of them, it's the first time they've taken to the streets for Palestine.

The Place de la République is packed with people. There's talk of 100,000 people. The mix of genres caught my attention. The regulars of the Palestinian cause are drowned in a diverse mass made up of left-wing organizations, trade unions, pacifists, feminists. There are bearded men and veiled women. Above all, there are a lot of young people. The suburbs are out in force. And so are the CRS. I leave the demonstration as night falls. I learn later that there was a bit of breakage at the end of the march.

On 18 January 2009, Israel announced that it had achieved its military objectives and declared an end to hostilities. A few hours later, Hamas declared itself victorious over the Israeli assault and announced its own ceasefire. Two days later, on the 20th, Barack Hussein Obama was sworn in on Capitol Square in Washington.

The new American president makes his first official phone call to Mahmoud Abbas, whose identity is no longer clear. La Sulta welcomes this first symbolic communication. Nothing has been done on either side to prevent the deaths of 1,330 Palestinians. Nor that of thirteen Israelis.

*

I finally returned to Ramallah almost a month later than originally planned. I've decided to stay at least until the summer. For the time being, I still have two weeks of work to do at the NSU. I also want to visit all those places I haven't yet had the chance to discover. Among them is a must-see in Israel: Yad Vashem. This visit was on my agenda when I arrived here. It's not too late now.

You arrive at the Yad Vashem memorial via a leafy road. Once the car has been parked in a brand-new parking lot, an elevator takes you to a wide, open esplanade. The air is fresh. The Jerusalem Forest is nearby. I stop for a moment to appreciate the pleasant surroundings. A colony of young soldiers is eating to my left. Some of them are basking in the sun, cigarettes in hand. Next to them, a low wall pays tribute to the main benefactors who helped build the memorial: Americans, Israelis, French, Australians, and Jews from all over the world contributed to its creation.

I'm at the gates of the temple of remembrance, surrounded by a gaggle of young Israelis, a bit of a rowdy bunch. I'm looking for the ticket office. I naively ask one of the employees where I should buy my ticket. As soon as I say these words, I realize how stupid I've been: it's sacrilegious to give a single cent to the guardians of the shrine that honours the dead of history's greatest genocide. Fortunately, the man I've spoken to takes no offense. He replies with a benevolent smile.

Further on, a small new wooden bridge leads to a massive, grey concrete building, like a newly erected block-house. The traverse spans a majestic pine forest. I take time to appreciate the view from the suspension bridge. My gaze would almost be lost in the tranquillity of the land-scape if I hadn't noticed some stone ruins. They're barely concealed by a few cypress trees. They are the remains of destroyed houses. They are the remains of a Palestinian village.[92] However, visitors to Yad Vashem have only one plaque to choose from. Hanging from the wooden bridge, it invites visitors to appreciate the scale of what awaits them:

'The bridge to a lost world built thanks to the generosity of Jan and Suzanne Czuker and their family (USA 2006).'

The lost Palestinian paradise is at my feet, just a few dozen meters away. I'm the only one to have spotted the traces of the village swallowed up by the Zionist dream. I turn, to my right, to my left. With deliberate steps, the

---

92. The Yad Vashem memorial is built on the site of two former Palestinian villages: Ein Kerem, part of which remains today, and the infamous Deir Yassin, which was wiped off the map on 9 April 1948 following massacres perpetrated by the Jewish militias of the Irgun and Lehi. Deir Yassin is considered one of the turning points in the first Arab–Israeli conflict, since it precipitated the Palestinian exodus and increased pressure on Arab leaders in neighbouring countries to intervene in the conflict.

students are about to begin their tour of the memorial. The blood rushes through my veins. I want to challenge them. I want to stop them. Point to the remains of the village. But to tell them what? These young Israelis aren't here to hear my story. They pass me by without a glance.[93]

I try to pull myself together. I take a deep breath. My gaze returns to the old stones. My eyes finally lift to appreciate the landscape as a whole. On the other side of the valley, a road and houses bear witness to another, Israeli, experience of life that has taken over.

I finally enter the grey concrete building. Triangular in shape, it is dimly lit, at least at the entrance. The building has two ends. On the first, the one now facing me, a film is being shown about Jewish life in Central and Eastern Europe in the first half of the twentieth century. At the opposite end, at the end of a winding path more than a hundred metres long, I can see daylight.

We're still a long way off. For the moment, my gaze is drawn to the projected black-and-white film about life in the *shtetl*[94] and to the motley crowd of Israeli teenagers, who linger like me in front of the projection. I get chills. The shattered Ashkenazi life, lost forever—its violins, songs, and prayers, its contrasts of grey, contrast with the

---

93. For the record, Yad Vashem dismissed one of its guides in April 2009. As he approached the ruins of the Palestinian village, he spoke to students at a Talmudic school about the Deir Yassin massacre. For further information: http://www.haaretz.com/hasen/spages/1080456.html
94. *Shtetl* is the Yiddish word for the small villages in Central and Eastern Europe where many Jews lived in the nineteenth century. These living quarters disappeared forever with the genocide perpetrated during the Second World War.

bright colours of the Israeli youth around me. The group is now attentive. I observe the boys and girls. Their faces, often with their southern, eastern, and African tones, are now all turned towards the tragic fate of European Jewry. Questions race through my mind. The torch, this burden they are taking on and which they will be given to pass on, must be immensely heavy to bear.

I'm continuing my visit. I've decided not to tell you about it. After a year in the occupied Palestinian territories, after Gaza, I'm not going to give you a detailed account of the emotions it inspired in me. The turmoil that the memorial brought out in me.

But I do invite you to visit. I strongly encourage you to do so. You must.

To understand.

Just promise me you'll also criss-cross occupied Palestine. From the Mediterranean to the Jordan. Palestine and Israel share a tragic destiny.

I realized it was inextricable.

XIII
ALLENBY BRIDGE
MARCH 1, 2009

It's 1 March 2009. I've just returned from an eight-day trip to the Gulf: a breath of air that's warmer than fresh, after a gruelling year. A visit to a few friends in Dubai, in particular, a little surreal and far removed from my current experience, did me a world of good.

A slightly too-early arrival at Amman airport doesn't dampen my enthusiasm: I'm going back home. I have just over three months to make up for lost time. My return ticket to Paris is scheduled for 8 June. I can't wait to finally enjoy the country, the countries, the people and what they have to offer. Because I'm still convinced that they have a lot to give, even if daily life likes to prove me wrong. I'm finally going to be able to 'enjoy.' The expression may not be appropriate to this troubled region. But that's the idea.

Jordan is rainy, almost flooded, after two days of incessant precipitation. My cab driver thanks God. To tell the truth, with my nose glued to the window, I'm not really listening to him. The landscape isn't beautiful. I'm daydreaming, absorbed in multiple projections of the weeks and months to come. My mind, now free of all constraints, wanders between my forthcoming return to Haifa and new walks in Galilee; the discovery of Jenin and Nazareth[95] too, and all those places I haven't yet seen. An encounter with Gaza, at last, I hope. I haven't given up hope.

Here I am at the King Hussein Bridge. *'Al jesser,'* as we say here. Or King Hussein Bridge. For once, I'm in luck: the border seems less crowded than usual. After a quick detour through Jordanian passport control and a cursory check of my luggage, I'm thrown onto a bus. It's already full and ready to leave for the Israeli border. Sorry—the border with the Israeli-controlled West Bank would be more accurate. We stop at the first passport control post within the Israeli-controlled buffer zone. We all get off the bus, show our passports to the officer in charge, then get back on the bus. I'm accompanied by a group of Japanese backpackers. Unshaven and haggard, they look completely lost. Next comes the traditional baggage drop-off for another check. It's far less chaotic than usual. There's none of the usual inhuman fair today.

For the first time at the Allenby Bridge[96] the experience is not unbearable. I can almost see a surprising attempt to regulate the flow of arrivals and their luggage. There's hope, I tell myself. Certainly, there are far fewer people. And the freshness of the air, softened by the rain, makes the

---

95. See "Israeltine" map, p. 225.
96. The crossing between the West Bank and Jordan, controlled by Israel, was named after Sir Edmund Allenby. A British officer and administrator, Allenby is known for having led the conquest of Palestine and Syria at the expense of the Ottomans during the Second World War.

exercise, the pushing of carts and elbowing, less painful than on previous occasions.

First interrogation. A young Israeli soldier, his English febrile but his posture firm, is helped by a more relaxed colleague. I answer all their questions, without hesitation. Clearly, I've had a bit of practice. I think I've mastered the exercise. I'm French, even if my interlocutors naturally stop at my Arabic first name. I explain what I do in Ramallah: I work as a legal advisor in the peace negotiations. Although these have been suspended for the time being, I'm still working on the same project. I won't mention my resignation. My former employer has agreed to cover for me. The Israeli Ministry of the Interior has been informed, so my arrival on Palestinian–Israeli soil should pose no difficulties.

I pass through an intimidating electronic air-jet machine whose purpose my Ramallah friends and I still haven't identified. After a reasonable wait, I present myself at the immigration counter. A young soldier, cute and visibly relaxed, welcomes me and asks me the usual questions. Her good mood is infectious. I let myself flirt a little. She smiles at me and hands me the usual form to fill in. I comply scrupulously, making sure to give the same information as usual. No more, no less: name, address, professional situation, reasons for my stay, and names and telephone numbers of my friends in Israel and the territories. After just over an hour, an Israeli Ministry of the Interior employee came to see me, passport in hand. The interview is brief. It was courteous. We go over the form together. He asks me to give him my cell phone number again. I do so without any problem.

Occupation seems more human to me today. Or perhaps I've integrated it for good, by dint of being around it. The new wait is a final, insignificant interlude. I'm happy to oblige by drinking a bracingly bad Turkish coffee.

An Israeli immigration employee jams her finger in the door of her counter. She screams. Two Palestinians, waiting like me, come over and ask about the state of the joint. I contemplate the scene from a distance, amused.

All in all, my wait since arriving at the Jordanian border took less than four hours. Record broken, hands down.

They call my name: Ziyaaad.'

I'd almost missed it. I present myself again at the counter where I'm to receive my long-awaited offering: my passport and a new three-month tourist visa. A soldier examines the document for a moment. She hands it to me:

'Ziyad, you can go, but we've been instructed to give you only a one-month visa.'

What the hell is she talking about? I sketch out a quizzical grin.

'Why?' I ask.
'You have to leave the territory.'

I pretend not to understand.

She tries to coax me with a smile.

'Don't cry, there's not that much to see in Israel anyway.'

An irrepressible sadness suddenly overcomes me. My eyes water. Just like that, in an instant, without me noticing. I freeze in place. The tears don't flow. The soldier, who has lost her smile, nods at me. It's unequivocal: she's ordering me to move forward. I'm pushed in the back: a Palestinian family. It's no longer my turn.

I move forward to join the last queue and retrieve my luggage. The farce is over. I thought I was nobody here; I thought I had nothing, yet something has been taken from me. I feel dispossessed.

*

A few months passed. I've left Israel and the Palestinian territories. I'm in London with my mother for a family reunion. This is where her own mother is buried. A native of Nazareth, once a Palestinian citizen in a country controlled by the British Crown, my grandmother rests here, far from Habib, far from Palestine, far from Lebanon. I tell my mother about my stay and its painful fall. My nerves are still raw.

She concludes, 'The Israelis took my father away from me, then my brother. They were fighting for their rights. They were condemned to exile. They died in exile. Then you left. To try and negotiate. Unsuccessfully. The circle is complete. They don't want to make peace.'

I remain silent. What I've been through doesn't allow me to contradict her.

I'm not much more forthcoming about what I learned there. Some things are even more painful to admit. The truth is that the Palestine of my grandfather and mother no longer exists. Only its fantasy remains.

The Israelis have won the battle of the land. But the Palestinians are still there, clinging to the ground that is slipping away beneath their feet. And a monster is born of the inability of these two peoples to make peace. Failing to characterize this incongruity of history born of two unfulfilled nationalist projects, I have resolved to call this reality 'Israeltine.' I now know that my roots are here and there, in Palestine, in Israel. Like many Palestinians. Like many Israelis. And, against the course of history, it is within this country, in its entirety, 'Israeltine,' that I claim my right to return.

*

"Israeltine"
(as of 2010)

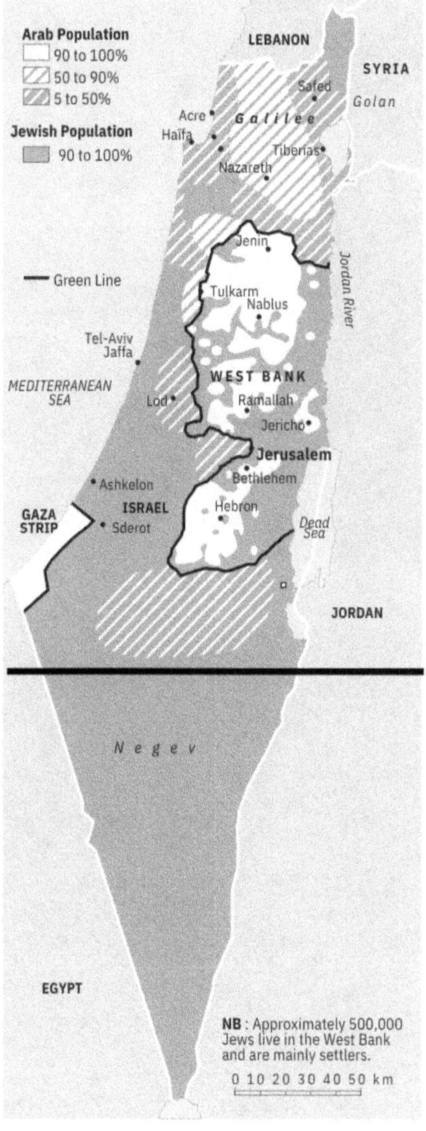

Allenby Bridge

APPENDICES

As just one example of the effort and money spent on an illusory "peace process", a round of Israeli–Palestinian negotiations gives rise to an unimaginable mass of documents of all kinds: notes, memos, minutes, action plans, language, minutes of meetings, chronologies, and so on.

Annapolis is no exception.

I have selected a handful of documents and reproduced them in the appendix, mainly to illustrate my own experience. My testimony is not intended to give an account of the infinite details of these talks. This work of journalism and investigation, important though it is, is not my own, and I accept that my account may be partial and subjective. In the five appendices that follow, I wanted to highlight two of the many shortcomings of this agonizing process that struck me the most. It seems to me that it is no longer possible to ignore them:

- The refugee question remains at the heart of Palestinian identity and the Israeli-Palestinian conflict (see appendices III and V). Along with Jerusalem, it remains the Gordian knot. However, the PLO, still negotiating under occupation 17 years after recognizing Israel, has gradually lost sight of the centrality of the fate of the majority of the Palestinian population still living in exile. Undermined by the explosion of colonization, the deterioration of daily life generated by the

Israeli occupation and its conflict with Hamas, it is no longer in a position to support the legitimate demands of the refugees. What's more, the growing imbalance in the Israeli-Palestinian balance of power makes the prospect of an equitable solution to this issue increasingly utopian for the Palestinians (appendices I and II).

- More generally, the leadership of the PLO and the Palestinian Authority, under pressure from Israel and the United States to be increasingly accommodating over the years, is today being led to censor itself, no longer duly asserting positions that are nonetheless validated by law and the international community (appendices III and IV). The loss of legitimacy of the PLO/Palestinian Authority is undoubtedly also to be found at this level: the Palestinian leadership in Ramallah is not only accountable to its people, but must also—if not more so, for its very survival—respond to the demands of its foreign supporters and backers (the United States and the European Union), as well as to the grievances of its natural interlocutor, the Israeli government. With rampant colonization, attrition and occupation continuing, the situation has long since become untenable.

The following documents have been reproduced in their original English versions. An introductory note precedes each document to summarize its content and clarify its scope.

APPENDIX I
ISRAEL'S FIRST DOCUMENT ON REFUGEES

This document is the first written proposal on refugees submitted by the Israeli negotiating delegation in April 2008 (cf. ch. VII "Haifa" pp. 111). This first offer reflects quite clearly the Israeli approach to the issue:

- The preamble to the proposed article essentially states that Israel and the PLO would recognize, with sadness, the suffering and losses endured on both sides by individuals, families and communities, including refugees (Palestinian? Jewish? The article deliberately fosters confusion.), as a result of their conflict. In other words, the fate of Palestinian refugees is seen on the Israeli side as a consequence, and by necessity one issue among others, of the Israeli–Palestinian conflict.

- Article 6.2 states that the resolution of this issue requires an "international effort". This reference reflects Israel's desire to shift as much of the burden of the Palestinian refugee problem as possible onto the international community. The second sentence of the article does however specify that "Israel accepts, for its part, the principle of a financial contribution to this resolution", which is a step forward. However, the article gives no information or guarantee as to the amount and payment of this contribution.

- Article 6.3 states that since the State of Palestine is destined to become the home of the Palestinian people, all refugees wishing to reside in Palestine will be entitled to Palestinian citizenship. The approach is implacably logical and rooted in the "two states for two peoples" vision promoted by President George W. Bush and endorsed by the Israeli negotiating delegation. In this scheme, the future of Palestinian refugees must lie exclusively in Palestine - or in the third countries where they currently reside. In other words, anywhere but Israel. However, this approach ignores the right of return as recognized by international law, and the limited absorption capacity of the "future Palestinian state", which could only enjoy a limited territory and resources.

- Article 6.5 testifies to the Israeli government's desire to see the United States assume leadership of the international mechanism that would manage the resolution of the Palestinian refugee question. For Israel, this solution would allow it to divest itself of responsibility for resolving the problem, while ensuring that its interests would continue to be protected by its natural ally, the United States.

-Nothing Agreed Until Everything Agreed-

In preamble:

Recognizing, with sorrow, the suffering and loss endured by individuals, families and communities on both sides, including refugees, as a result of the conflict between them;

Article 6 Refugees

6.1 The Parties recognize the urgent need, in the context of realizing the two State vision, to address and resolve the refugee issue in accordance with the terms of the Agreement.

6.2 The Parties recognize that the resolution of the refugee issue will require an international effort. Israel, for its part, will contribute financially to this effort, in accordance with the Article.

6.3 Recognizing that the State of Palestine shall be the homeland of the Palestinian people, all Palestinian refugees wishing to reside in Palestine shall be entitled to Palestinian citizenship

----

6.5 In order to enable a comprehensive, organized and conclusive settlement of the refugee issue, the Parties have invited the United States, in coordination with them, to establish and lead an international refugee mechanism which will operate in accordance with the provisions of this Article.

Mechanism principles... (subsequent meeting)

APPENDIX II
PALESTINIAN *"NON-PAPER"* ON REFUGEES

The document submitted to the Israelis following the proposal reproduced in Appendix I does not, strictly speaking, constitute a counter-offer (cf. ch. VII "Haifa" pp. 111). It does, however, reflect the PLO's approach to refugees, which has also been endorsed by all Arab and Muslim countries as part of the Arab Peace Initiative. It is in line with the rights of refugees as recognized by international law. It goes even further, since it introduces a compromise on the question of the return of refugees to Israel: this will take place according to a limited quota and periodicity accepted by Israel. In other words, the PLO wants the right of return to be recognized in principle, but is willing to place limits on its implementation.

For the rest, the rights of Palestinian refugees under international law can be summarized as follows:

- recognition of Israel's responsibility for creating and perpetuating the refugee problem;

- implementation of the right to return *through* the various options available to refugees (repatriation, integration in host countries and settlement in third countries);

- restitution and/or full compensation for material and immaterial damage suffered by refugees, including loss of opportunity and human rights violations resulting from their forced and prolonged exile.

Finally, the resolution of the refugee problem will be achieved *through the* establishment of an international mechanism whose mandate will extend to the implementation of all these rights as stipulated in the peace agreement. An international fund will be set up to finance the various programs managed by the international mechanism.

At the same time, the "host states" that took in Palestinian refugees will have to be compensated.

- NON-PAPER -

For Discussion Purposes

Article 6 Refugees

6.1. The Parties commit to pursue a comprehensive, just and agreed upon resolution of the Palestinian refugee problem as envisaged by the Arab Peace Initiative, and in accordance with international law and the terms of the Article:

6.2.1 Israel acknowledges its moral and legal responsibility for the longstanding displacement and dispossession of the Palestinian civilian population stemming from its actions during and subsequent to the War of 1948.

6.2.2 Refugees shall be provided with repatriation and resettlement options, including return to Israel - to be implemented in accordance with an agreed annual quota and within an agreed period of time (renewable on the basis of both parties' consent) -, and return to Palestine, as its sole discretion.

6.2.3 Refugees shall be granted restitution and/or full compensation for the material and non-material damages they have suffered, including loss of opportunities and human rights suffering as a result of their protracted displacement.

6.2.4 States that have hosted Palestinian refugees shall be entitled for remuneration.

6.3 In order to enable a comprehensive, just and effective settlement of the refugee issue, an international mechanism shall be established to implement all aspects of the Treaty relating to refugees with the participation of Palestine, Israel, the host countries and other necessary and willing countries and entities.

6.4 In furtherance thereof, an international fund shall be established to finance the repatriation, resettlement and rehabilitation of the refugee, and the reparation program, including restitution and/or compensation. Israel commits to contribute financially to the fund as to be agreed in the Treaty, along with the contributions from responsible third states.

Appendix III
President Abbas' draft platform for the sixtieth commemoration of the Nakba

It was to be signed by President Mahmoud Abbas and published in the international press on May 15, 2008, the date of the Nakba commemoration. Abbas had given the go-ahead. The article was not published, however, for fear that the PLO would alienate its negotiating partners: Israel and the Americans. The PLO thus missed the chance to put Palestinian refugees back at the heart of the peace talks (cf. ch. VIII "Nakba" pp. 127).

However, the text is very moderate. After briefly evoking his experience as a refugee (Abu Mazen had to flee his hometown, Safad[97] to Syria in 1948), the PLO leader recalls that his fate was shared by hundreds of thousands of Palestinians, many of whom still live in camps. While Palestinian refugees today make up the world's largest refugee population (seven million), the text stresses that this situation contributes to the instability of the Middle East. The Palestinian people are still suffering from a sense of injustice: they are still waiting for their history to be recognized, an indispensable condition for achieving a real and lasting peace between equals. Abbas, noting that the Arab peace initiative is still on the table, therefore invites Israel to acknowledge its responsibility for the fate of the Palestinian refugees. Far from weakening the Hebrew state, such recognition would enable

---

97. See "Israeltine" map, p. 225.

both Israeli and Palestinian parties, their leaders and their peoples, to emerge strengthened in their efforts for peace, and to embark on the road to historic reconciliation.

As a sign of the moderation of this text, at no point does the forum refer to the right of return.

This week Israel celebrates its 60th anniversary since its formation on May 15, 1948. For Palestinians, today marks the 60th year since the "Nakba" - our national and personal catastrophe, involving the loss of our ancestral homeland and the dispersal of three-quarters of our people into exile. To date, the Palestinian people await Israeli recognition of its responsibility in the catastrophe and agreement to resolve the conflict based on international law, including UN resolutions.

I experienced exile first-hand. On May 12, 1948 two days before Israel's declaration of independence, my hometown of Safed was captured by Jewish forces. 10,000 Palestinian inhabitants of the town were forced to leave. I was 13. My family and I fled by foot to Syria. We were never allowed to return.

The same reality befell more than 726,000 indigenous Christian and Muslim Palestinians who fled their homes or were expelled from Mandate Palestine in and around 1948; while hundreds of Palestinians were killed.

In the wake of the expulsion, more than 418 Palestinian villages were razed to the ground. Nearly all Palestinian property, including that belonging to Palestinians who managed to stay within the areas that came under Israeli control, was confiscated by the nascent State of Israel for the exclusive benefit of Jews. In 1952, when Israel's parliament passed its nationality law, Palestinian refugees were denied the option of citizenship in the new state. Additional measures were taken to bar our return to our country and our homes. The expulsion of Palestinians and the subsequent measures to render the displacement permanent were taken in contravention of international law.

These events, which left the majority of Palestinians stateless and dispossessed, were compounded by the Israeli military occupation of the West Bank and Gaza Strip in 1967. Hundreds of thousands of Palestinians once again fled their homes, and Israel expanded its control over the remaining 22% of our historic homeland. Today, the stranglehold over the Gaza Strip, the ongoing settlement and closure activities in the West Bank, including East Jerusalem, is leading to more Palestinian fragmentation and displacement. Indeed, the "Nakba" continues.

Today, there are more than 7 million Palestinian refugees. They constitute the largest refugee population in the world and one of the world's longest unresolved refugee crises. Palestinian refugee vulnerability, brought about as a result of their protracted mass exile and statelessness, is contributing to Middle East regional instability and insecurity, from Iraq to Lebanon to the Gaza Strip.

As a Palestinian, I cannot forget the uprooting of my nation, which has shaped my history and which has created the continuation of a reality of hardship for my people. At the same time, Palestinians have expressed their desire to achieve conciliation and move forward based on an accommodation grounded in the acknowledgement and just implementation of our rights.

In the course of the 60 years since the Palestinian "Nakba", Israel's responsibility for the forced displacement and dispossession of the Palestinian people has been clearly established by historians (many of them Israelis) and international legal scholars. The right of individual Palestinians to choose whether to return to their homes and determine their own destinies has continued to be reaffirmed by the international community in UN General Assembly Resolution 194. Yet, this historical injustice remains officially unacknowledged and the human rights of Palestinians denied.

I profoundly regret that Israel continues to disregard the Arab Peace Initiative (API), adopted by the Arab League in Beirut in

March 2002. The API calls for an independent Palestinian state in the West Bank and Gaza Strip along the pre-1967 borders, with East Jerusalem as its capital, and a just solution to the Palestinian refugee problem to be agreed upon in accordance with UNGA Resolution 194, in exchange for normalization of relations with Israel and a lasting peace. The API has been repeatedly reaffirmed by Arab countries, including this past March in Damascus. Additionally, the Organization of the Islamic Conference (OIC) which represent 57 Islamic countries worldwide has endorsed the API as the basis to end the Arab/Palestinian Israeli conflict. What this means, in practical terms, is achieving peace between Israel and more than 1 Billion Arabs and Muslims worldwide.

Peace is made between equals, through the respect of each side's history and identity, and understanding the discourse of the "Other". As history proves, States commit wrongs, but States are strengthened when they acknowledge and apologize for those wrongs. To end the denial, the suffering, and the resentment that has led to violence and conflict, to reach the accommodation proposed by the Arab Peace Initiative and President Bush's vision of the two-state solution living side by side in peace and security, it is necessary that the Palestinians be recognized as dignified human beings entitled to the same treatment and laws as other refugees and victims of conflict.

To achieve real peace, it will be necessary for Israel to acknowledge its responsibility in the creation and perpetuation of the plight of the refugees. Such an acknowledgement is not a threat to its existence. It is in fact the exact opposite. By doing so, Israel would inevitably empower our respective citizens and leadership to establish peace based on political accommodation.

I am committed to the permanent status negotiations with Israel launched in Annapolis in November 2007 as I see no viable alternative to dialogue and agreement for resolving the injustice and misery that the Palestinians have suffered for 60 years.

Today, the 15th of May 2008, remains for Palestinians a day of sadness, sorrow, and longing.

On the 60th commemoration of the Palestinian "Nakba", I invite Israel to acknowledge its responsibilities, recognize our rights and suffering, and work with us for a breakthrough for peace, historical reconciliation, and an end of conflict.

When this happens, we will all celebrate together.

Appendix IV
Draft letter from the Palestinian negotiators to US Secretary of State C. Rice

Like Appendix III, this letter illustrates the self-censorship now practiced by Palestinian negotiators (cf. ch. ix "Negotiations" pp. 141). After six months of the "peace process", the situation on the ground is dramatic: the blockade on Gaza has been tightened, military incursions into Palestinian territory are multiplying, and settlement activity is exploding, with its attendant destruction of Palestinian homes and expropriations.

At the negotiating table, no progress: while the Palestinians do not hesitate to put their positions in writing on the table, they come up against a wall on the Israeli side. As summarized in the letter reproduced below, the Palestinian and Israeli delegations differ fundamentally in their approach to the talks: while the Palestinians try to define the objective to be achieved and the best way to get there, the Israelis start from the situation prevailing on the ground and agree at best to negotiate some limited and gradual improvements to the status quo.

As early as June 2008, the NSU tried to convince the leadership of the Palestinian negotiating delegation that it was necessary to report the situation to Condoleezza Rice, so that she would be able to understand the reasons preventing the talks from moving forward. The letter is prepared with this in mind. It takes stock of Israeli actions that are obstacles to the creation of an independent, viable and sovereign Palestinian state. It details the Palestinian position on each of the permanent status issues.

This missive was amended more than a dozen times between June and August 2008. After much prevarication, the PLO finally decided not to hand it over to the Americans, once again for fear of "offending" its ally...

In September 2008, Israeli Prime Minister Ehud Olmert had no qualms about claiming that the negotiations had failed due to a lack of courage on the part of the Palestinians.

June 15th, 2008

Dear Secretary Rice;

On the occasion of today's trilateral meeting, we would like to present to you our assessment of the current status of negotiations and our vision for the way forward. We recognize and appreciate the commitment that both President Bush and you have made towards helping to reach our common goals of two states based on the 1967 borders, living side by side in peace and security, and a just resolution to the refugee issue.

We have reached an important point in the negotiations; on some issues we have achieved some progress, but there remain many gaps and difficulties. As you know, the issues before us are extremely sensitive and difficult, all the more so given ongoing Israeli policies and practices, such as construction of the Wall on Palestinian land, continued settlement expansion and the intensification of the internal closure regime.

In short, we are facing two major difficulties in our negotiations with Israel. <u>First</u>, our **negotiations approaches** are fundamentally different. While <u>our goal is</u> to define where we want to go up front, namely to establish an independent sovereign state based on 1967 borders with all the rights and responsibilities that it entails, and to have a just resolution to the refugee issue, <u>the Israeli approach</u> is to start with the current situation and negotiate small and gradual improvements to the status quo. This allows Israel to use "security" as a catch-all to derogate from Palestinian sovereignty in a permanent status agreement.

Palestinians want the same rights and responsibilities enjoyed by other states, no more and no less: full sovereignty with all its attributes, including full control of our airspace, maritime space, territory, borders, water, electromagnetic sphere and other resources.

Any proposal that merely consolidates unilaterally imposed facts on the ground, or results in a "state with provisional borders", would necessarily contradict our fundamental rights and interests and would not be acceptable. The Palestinian people cannot be expected to acquiesce to a slightly improved version of the occupation that is then repackaged as a "state".

<u>Second</u>, as you know, Israel continues to build in and expand settlements on Palestinian territory in a manner which is meant to prejudge the outcome of permanent status negotiations. By continuing settlement activities, and building roads and other infrastructure throughout the West Bank, particularly in and around East Jerusalem, Israel is undermining the current negotiations, as well as the credibility of negotiating parties, the United States and the international community. More importantly, such activities threaten the viability of an independent sovereign Palestinian state and will soon spell the death of the two-state solution.

In the months since Annapolis, Israel has continued its assault on Palestinian national and individual rights, in violation of international law, while showing flagrant disregard for virtually all of its obligations under the Road Map. Construction has continued in at least 101 settlements (not including Jerusalem-area settlements). Similarly, Israeli authorities have issued tenders for 1,731 new housing units since Annapolis, which is already more than 12 times the number of housing units tendered in the 12 months prior to Annapolis. Meanwhile, Israeli authorities demolished at least 185 Palestinian structures, including 85 homes, in the first four months after Annapolis. The number of checkpoints, roadblocks and other physical barriers to movement now exceeds 600. And, of course, Israel has yet to comply with the 2004 ruling of the International Court of Justice, which held that the settlements and the Wall that are built in the Occupied Palestinian Territory (OPT) are illegal, and which requires Israel to stop constructing the Wall, remove those parts already built and provide reparations.

Throughout all our meetings and negotiations we have never stopped demanding that Israel stop its ongoing violations with respect to the Wall, the settlements, the closure, the incursions into Palestinian territory, the demolitions, etc. Throughout the negotiations, Israel has in fact intensified its violations, as demonstrated by the figures noted above. These ongoing violations deprive our meetings and negotiations of credibility, and prevent the process from gaining the necessary support of the Palestinian people.

In any case, we have entrusted you, Secretary Rice, to facilitate these negotiations towards our common goals of the realization of two states based on the 1967 borders, living side by side in peace and security, and to a just resolution to the refugee issue and to assist us all in finding a constructive way forward that ensures that the interests and needs of both parties are satisfied. In furtherance of this goal, we outline below for you the status, as we see it, of each of the core issues currently being discussed in these negotiations.

Terms of Reference

Although we've agreed to several ground rules for the negotiations, we have yet to agree to the terms of reference by which any agreement will be governed.

The four key elements of the ground rules have been that:

1. Nothing is agreed until everything is agreed;

2. We will not involve the media in the discussions, and will keep all substantive aspects of the discussions completely confidential;

3. We will discuss all core permanent status issues, including Borders, Jerusalem, Refugees, Water, Settlements and Security; and

4. We are working towards a comprehensive agreement.

On the terms of reference, however, there is significantly less agreement. While Israel would like minimal terms of reference and relies heavily on agreeing to bilateral arrangements in a vacuum, we continue to insist on the universally accepted terms of reference for this conflict. Our baseline and terms of reference are those that the international community and international law have established, namely that any agreement must be based on the United Nations resolutions pertinent to the conflict, specifically UNSC 242, 338, 252 and 478 the Road Map as endorsed in UNSC Res. 1515, and the Arab Peace Initiative of 2002, reaffirmed in 2007; it must be based on international law; the agreement, based on the "land for peace" formula, must lead to the end of the Israeli occupation that began in 1967 and end the conflict, thus establishing an independent viable and sovereign Palestinian State; and resolving the issue of the refugees in a just and agreed upon manner, in accordance with UNGA 194.

Territory

The Palestinian position is, and has always been, that the two state solution must be based on the 1967 border, which defines the borders of West Bank, including East Jerusalem, the Jordan Valley, the No Man's Land (including in the Latrun), and the Dead Sea, and the Gaza Strip. We are content with the 1967 line, which is the universally accepted baseline for the border. However, we are willing to consider minor modifications to the 1967 line, if those modifications satisfy Palestinian rights and interests, are on the basis of one-to-one land swaps equal in quality and size, which should not exceed 1.9% of the total area of the West Bank (including East Jerusalem) and the Gaza Strip.

Moreover, it is important to bear in mind that the percentage of swap alone, while important, is not a sufficient basis by which to evaluate the reasonableness of a proposal. We cannot accept any proposal that severs East Jerusalem from the rest of Palestine, harms Palestinian contiguity, involves the swap of Palestinians (regardless of their citizenship) or otherwise harms core Palestinian interests as determined by the PLO. In addition, we do not accept the concept of so called "settlement blocs", much less accept their wholesale annexation. We will only address possible swaps on a settlement by settlement basis. It is for these reasons that the settlements of Ariel, Givat Zeev, Ma'ale Adumim, Har Homa, Efrat will not be considered under any scenario.

The Palestinian proposal is in stark contrast to that of the Israeli side, which has refused to present a complete map (that includes Jerusalem) and has put forward a maximal proposal that undermines Palestinian viability, creates enclaves, and encompasses vast amounts of our vacant land and water productive areas. Their proposal largely mirrors the path of the Wall, which they had repeatedly assured the international community would not be used to pre-determine the border! In short, the map that Israel has thus far proposed in the discussions is incomplete, and does not address even the most basic Palestinian rights. It proposes annexing 7.3% of the West Bank (according to Israel's own calculations), in a manner which totally undermines the viability of the future state of Palestine, particularly with respect to the future of Jerusalem, and does not address Israel's territorial aspirations in Jerusalem at all.

In exchange, Prime Minister Olmert has offered the equivalent of 5% of Israeli territory in the desert areas adjacent to the southern West Bank and the northern part of the Gaza Strip. Prime Minister Olmert has also suggested as part of the "compensation" for the swap, Palestine would get a dock at Ashdod port, *in lieu of our own sovereign port in the Gaza Strip*, as well as a territorial link between the West Bank and the Gaza Strip under Israeli sovereignty but purportedly under full, uninterrupted and complete Palestinian control.

To summarize, any discussion on borders must address the border as a whole, including in Jerusalem, without gaps or omissions. A piecemeal approach will neither meet the interests of both sides, nor result in an acceptable border. Therefore, it will not be possible to agree on a final border whilst Israel refuses to put forward a more reasonable proposal, which must include its vision for Jerusalem and for swaps on its side of the 1967 line.

Jerusalem

Jerusalem is the key to successful negotiations. The realization of Palestinian rights and sovereignty in East Jerusalem, as the capital of the Palestinian state, is essential to any lasting peace agreement.

Appendices

Postponing the issue of Jerusalem (or agreeing to a border that excludes Jerusalem) would not be credible, realistic or acceptable, since this would merely allow Israel to continue creating additional facts on the ground. Moreover, it is illogical to believe that an issue as difficult as Jerusalem is today would be anything but more difficult later.

Although we have put forward our position on Jerusalem several times, Israel has yet to present anything meaningful on the issue. In order for us to reach an agreement, it must be comprehensive and must address all issues.

On Jerusalem, although sovereignty must be divided along the 1967 lines (with whatever modifications are agreed to as part of swaps, in accordance with the above principles and not including sites holy to Muslims or Christians), modalities may be agreed to that do not necessarily conform to the same lines.

Palestinians are tied to Jerusalem through strong historic, moral, religious, social and economic links. These links cannot be severed without significant economic and social hardship which will in turn generate greater instability within East Jerusalem, and within the West Bank as a whole.

Despite its clear obligation under Phase I of the Road Map, Israel continues to reject calls by the Quartet and the international community to reopen Palestinian institutions in East Jerusalem. The immediate reopening of Orient House and other Palestinian institutions would serve as a critical first step to rebuilding Palestinian trust and confidence in Israel's desire for peace and in the peace process and its seriousness in addressing all core issues.

Water

There is a fundamental disagreement between the Palestinian and Israeli approaches to resolving the issue of water. Palestinians insist that the only reasonable first step is to determine the issue of both parties' water rights - the Palestinian and Israeli percentage of the shared conventional water resources determined in accordance with international law - regardless of the available amount of shared groundwater and surface water year to year. Only then can the parties turn to discussing methods of cooperation to maximize existing water resources for both parties. To fully consider their respective water rights consistent with accepted international practice, the parties must analyze and discuss all shared transboundary watercourses (surface and ground waters), including the Jordan River, which Israel refuses to consider for political reasons.

In contrast to the Palestinian approach, Israel refuses to engage in any discussion of water rights and frames the negotiations in terms of regional water scarcity with the view to cooperate on extending use of current allocations through wastewater treatment, as well as developing new non-conventional sources of water.

Finally, it is important to note, at the June 12, 2008 meeting of the Trilateral Water Committee chaired by the United States, members of the Israeli delegation put forward an interpretation of the Oslo Interim Agreement asserting that the additional 80 Million cubic meters of water agreed and to be developed by the Palestinians under the agreement reflects future Palestinian needs regardless of the interim period. Thus, the Israeli position is that allocations and development of additional waters under the Interim Agreement are to be the *de facto* permanent status allocations, regardless of our actual water rights or long-term needs.

Refugees

The issue of the refugees is one of the core issues of the conflict: without its just resolution, there can be no end of conflict. Any agreement that does not address the issue of refugees completely and comprehensively, in accordance with international law and international best standards, would be just another interim agreement and would only prolong the conflict.

There are four aspects to the issue of refugees. First, Israel's **recognition of responsibility** for the creation and perpetuation of the problem is a crucial part of any solution in order to give people a sense of satisfaction that their overall historical experience have been acknowledged and addressed and to facilitate any possible compromise on implementation, and is therefore essential to enable the establishment of a *real* peace with Palestinian refugees. Israel thus far has refused to recognize its responsibility with respect to the issue of the refugees.

Second, although we understand that full implementation of the **right of return** is unlikely, in order for there to be a solution, the return option will have to be perceived as a real option. The right of return is a recognized right under international law and it has been a core aspect of the Palestinian struggle for the last 60 years. Therefore, it must be addressed in a reasonable manner that takes into account the existence of this individual right, its centrality in refugee experience, as well as Israel's capacity of absorption. As the PLO, we are not the holder of refugees' individual rights but we have a mandate to pursue the recognition and implementation of these rights, and can only seek to maximize the choices for the refugees. Israel thus far has insisted that refugees be entitled to Palestinian citizenship and/or provided with resettlement and integration options only (no return to Israel).

Third, on **reparations**, the Palestinian position remains that refugees shall be granted restitution and compensation for the material and non material damages they have suffered (including loss of livelihood and opportunities and human suffering, as a result of refugees' protracted displacement). Therefore, compensation is only one part of reparations due. In addition, states that have hosted Palestinian refugees shall be entitled to remuneration. Israel thus far has been willing to consider only compensation for the refugees. Their position on the other aspects of reparations remains unclear.

Finally, the **international implementation mechanism** must include all of the stakeholders that are part of the implementation

There Will Be No Palestinian State

process in order for it to work effectively. The international community will have to be represented in the mechanism to guarantee the efficiency and durability of the implementation process. In addition, all of its aspects must be agreed (in other words it must have full parameters) in order for it to be operational. Israel agrees to an international implementation mechanism.

Security

As regards security, we have presented reasonable and flexible proposals in response to the blanket demand for "full demilitarization" by Israel. In short, we have made clear that we are willing to look at any fair solution to meet Israeli security interests *short of a continued Israeli presence on Palestinian territory*. More specifically, we have said that Palestine will be a sovereign, independent state with limited arms— not limited dignity. As a sovereign and independent state, Palestine will have sovereignty and full control over its territory, including airspace and territorial waters.

To meet our internal security needs, our security forces will need all appropriate weapons and equipment to perform their duties and responsibilities. We have agreed to a third party role to take care of our defense needs for a limited agreed period.

However, following decades of Israeli military occupation, Palestine cannot accept any Israeli military presence or control over its territory whatsoever. Our people will not buy into any agreement that includes a continuation of Israeli control over their land. Israel continues to insist on a presence in Palestinian territory, post-agreement, and has thus far been unwilling to accept a third party role that would be more extensive than that of purely capacity building.

Prisoners

The signature of an agreement resolving the permanent status issues between Palestinians and Israelis will mark a historic reconciliation, and as such, all Palestinian and Arab prisoners detained or arrested by Israel as a result of the Israeli-Palestinian conflict must be released. While Israel has not presented a formal position on this matter, it has agreed to discuss this issue in the current round of negotiations.

The Israeli approach shows that Israel is trying to secure our agreement for a state with provisional borders, or some form of protectorate or trusteeship, and to call that a "state". This, as you can imagine, is not, and will never be, acceptable to us; nor would it end the conflict. In order for the conflict between us and the Israeli government to be ended, an agreement must be just, comprehensive and address the interests of both sides.

With this letter, we ask you to kindly assist us in reaching a peace agreement; one that is sustainable and lasting and that will finally end this decades-long conflict.

Please accept, Madame Secretary, the expression of my highest consideration.

Sincerely,

Ahmed Qurie

Head of Palestinian Delegation

to Permanent Status Negotiations

H.E. Condoleezza Rice

Secretary of State

Washington, DC

Cc:

Foreign Minister Tzipi Livni

APPENDIX V
OPEN LETTER FROM 78 PALESTINIAN NGOS AND FACTIONS TO PRESIDENT ABBAS ON REFUGEE RIGHTS AND ONGOING NEGOTIATIONS

The letter reproduced below was delivered to the office of President Mahmoud Abbas on behalf of 78 Palestinian civil society organizations, from the territories and the Diaspora, on Monday September 22, 2008. All Palestinian factions, including Fatah and Hamas, have signed the document (cf. ch. x "The generous offer" pp. 173).

The petition has been prepared in response to concerns that negotiations with Israel on the refugee issue are being pursued without any consultation with the refugees, and in view of the pressure being put on Palestinian negotiators on this particular issue.

This letter is the clearest proof yet that refugees and the right to return remain at the heart of the Palestinian identity. There can be no doubt that a peace agreement will be judged by the justice rendered to the first victims of this conflict, the Palestinian refugees. What other document could today bear the signatures of Fatah and Hamas alongside dozens of Palestinian organizations and associations based in the territories, the Arab world, Europe and America?

The petition recalls the inalienable and historic rights of Palestinian refugees. It also expresses the concerns of Palestinian civil society representatives about the current round of negotiations, and calls on Palestinian negotiators to open up to refugee organizations about developments in the talks, in order to strengthen their positions on this issue.

Open Letter to President Mahmoud Abbas

To: President Mahmoud Abbas

Chair of the Palestine Liberation Organization Executive Committee

President of the Palestinian National Authority

CC:

League of Arab States

Non-Aligned Movement

Organization of the Islamic Conference

Re: The Rights of Palestinian Refugees

and the Final Status Negotiations

Dear Mr. President,

Greetings of Return

We, the undersigned Palestinian refugee organizations, civil society movements and institutions in the Palestinian homeland and in exile are national organizations working to defend the right of return. We appeal to you now because we are convinced that the alignment of the official Palestinian position and the position of the Palestinian people with regards to the final status negotiation issues is of the highest priority. Foremost among these issues is the cause of the Palestinian refugees.

We are convinced that the alignment of popular and official positions is the main guarantee of a strong Palestinian position in the current negotiation process, which is taking place in a local, regional and global context that jeopardizes the national rights of the Palestinian people. In this context, we are concerned in particular about the rights of Palestinian refugees and internally displaced persons to return to their original lands and properties, restitution of their homes, lands and properties and compensation for damages incurred over the past 60 years. Based on the fact that all of these rights are guaranteed under international law, and based on our awareness of the enormous pressures faced by Palestinian negotiators and the tactics of negotiations, such as secrecy with regards to the negotiation proceedings, we call upon you to adopt a negotiation strategy that is based on openness with the entirety of the Palestinian people - irrespective of their current place of residence - regarding all aspects and details of the negotiation process. Implementation of the Palestinian refugees' right of return was and continues to be the main purpose for which the Palestine Liberation Organization (PLO) was established, a purpose which forms the central pillar of the PLO's legitimacy as the sole legitimate representative of the Palestinian people. Transparency and candidness of our representatives with all sectors of our society will guarantee that our rights are best defended, and strengthen our position in the face of enormous pressures.

It has been clear at all stages of the negotiations that this process aims to eliminate the core issue of the Arab/Palestinian struggle for freedom and justice: the Palestinian refugees and their rights of return and restitution. In fact, elimination of these central Palestinian/ Arab demands form the center-piece of both Israeli and US policies. It is also no secret that during the so-called "Oslo Peace Process" these policies have employed insidious tactics in order to nullify these rights altogether. Such tactics include attempts to substitute the return and restitution of the refugees with monetary compensation; to reduce the number of those entitled to exercise these rights from over 7 million Palestinian refugees and internally displaced persons to a tiny minority, including so-called "hardship cases" that would be arbitrarily defined by Israel; to suggest that the refugees return to homes located in the areas administered by the Palestinian Authority; and other humiliating "trade-offs" whereby Palestinians are expected to surrender the right of refugees to return to homes, lands and properties of origin in exchange for other rights and demands, such as self-determination, borders, the reclamation of Jerusalem and removal of the illegal settlement-colonies. The Palestinian leadership has rejected such degrading bargaining tactics in previous negotiations, notably those known as the second Camp David summit and the Clinton initiative. The late President Yasser Arafat rejected these tactics, and he was made to pay for that with his liberty and his life.

Whereas the rights of return, restitution and compensation are enshrined in international law and specifically affirmed in UN General Assembly Resolution 194 and UN Security Council Resolution 237;

Whereas we see that increasing US pressure aims to force Palestinian negotiators to agree to an obscure framework for a solution that is to be achieved by any means and at the soonest date, and that such a framework is largely for internal US consumption in the context of a US Presidential election;

Whereas it has become clear that the US administration is working on other fronts to market its obscure framework for a solution in the September 2008 session of the UN General Assembly;

Whereas we realize, as a result of our movement's long and difficult experience with Israeli politics, that Israeli political actors seek to solve the internal Israeli political crisis by venting destruction on the Palestinian front through various policies and practices, all of which work to entrench Israeli occupation, colonialism, and apartheid, and aim to attain international recognition of Israel as a 'Jewish State;'

Whereas Western and Israeli election platforms must not be employed to put pressure on the Palestinian negotiators, who should in no way be a party to the political maneuvers of US and Israeli political candidates, particularly in order to protect the legality, legitimacy, and sanctity of Palestinian national rights regardless of who emerges victorious in foreign elections;

Whereas we perceive the retreat of the once principled European position, and the transformation of this position into one that conforms to the US policy of total complicity and support for Israel;

Whereas we clearly see the weakness and inability of the Arab countries to take action or play any effective role;

Whereas we witness the sharp, painful and unprecedented deterioration in the internal Palestinian political arena;

Whereas it has become plain and obvious that powerful external pressures aim to annul Palestinian refugee rights, particularly the right to return to their original lands and properties and the restitution of these lands and properties;

Whereas Israel and the US, according to Israeli officials, are intensifying their efforts to reach a framework for a solution that is acceptable to both Israel and the US and will be viable regardless of the ruling party;

Whereas the primary measure of the legitimacy of any solution remains the extent to which it will lead to the exercise of the right of self-determination by the Palestinian people, including foremost the right of Palestinian refugees to choose to return to their original homes and lands regardless of their current place of refuge,

We approach you with this statement based on our strong desire to chart a way forward that is built on the highest levels of clarity and candidness with the Palestinian people; a way forward that aims to strengthen the Palestinian position in this sensitive stage of the Palestinian struggle; a way forward that ensures that any framework for a solution will include the following principles in clear and immutable language:

1. The rights of Palestinian refugees and internally displaced persons to return, restitution and compensation are fundamental

rights under international law and relevant UN resolutions - particularly UN General Assembly Resolution 194 and UN Security Council Resolution 237. The content of these rights is non-negotiable irrespective of the manner in which they will be exercised;

2. The right of return is an individual right held by every Palestinian refugee and internally displaced person. This right is passed on from one generation to the next, based on the individual's choice on whether or not to return, an inalienable and indivisible right, and not affected by any bilateral, multilateral, or international treaty or agreement. Any such agreement must respect the fundamental precepts and principles of international law;

3. The right of Palestinian refugees and internally displaced persons to return is a collective right that is not limited to one group or another, and it is an integral part of the Palestinian right of self-determination;

4. The right of Palestinian refugees and internally displaced persons to return is not subject to referendum.

May you remain steadfast in our struggle for freedom and dignity

Signed:

1. 194 Association (Syria)

2. Abassiya Association (Palestine)

3. Abnaa Al-Balad Center for the Defense of the Right of Return (Syria)

4. Aidun Group (Lebanon)

5. Aidun Group (Syria)

6. Al-Awda Palestine Network (Holland)

7. Al-Awda Palestine Right to Return Coalition (North America)

8. Arab Cultural Forum (Gaza, Palestine)

9. Arab Liberation Front

10. Arab Palestinian Front

11. Association for the Defense of the Rights of the Internally Displaced (Palestine)

12. Badil Resource Center for Palestinian Residency and Refugee Rights (Palestine)

13. Beit Nabala Association (Palestine)

14. Bisan Association (Syria)

15. Coalition of Right of Return Defense Committees (Jordan)

16. Coalition of Right of Return Defense Committees (Jordan)

17. Committee for the Rights of Palestinian Women (Syria)

18. Confederation of Right of Return Committees (Europe: Denmark, Sweden, Norway, Switzerland, Greece, Germany, France, Holland, Poland, Finland)

19. Coordinating Committee of Palestinian Organizations Working in Lebanon (Lebanon)

20. Council of National and Islamic Forces in Palestine (Palestine)

21. Democratic Front for the Liberation of Palestine

22. Democratic Palestine Committee

23. Depopulated Towns and Villages Associations (Gaza, Palestine)

24. Farah Heritage Society (Syria)

25. Grassroots Palestinian Anti-Apartheid Wall Campaign (Palestine)

26. Higher Follow-up Committee on Prisoners (Palestine)

27. Higher National Committee for the Defense of the Right of Return (Palestine)

28. Inevitable Return Assembly (Syria)

29. Islamic Jihad Movement

30. Islamic Resistance Movement [Hamas]

31. Istiqlal Youth Union (Lebanon)

32. Istiqlal Youth Union (Syria)

33. Ittijah: Union of Palestinian Non-Governmental Organizations (Palestine)

34. Jafra Youth Center (Syria)

35. Jimzo Association (Palestine)

36. Lajee Center, Aida Camp (Palestine)

37. National Assembly of Palestinian Civil Society Organizations (Palestine)

38. National Committee to Commemorate the Martyr Ahmad Al-Shuqairy (Jordan)

39. National Nakba Commemoration Committee (Palestine)

40. Palestine Democratic Union [Fida]

41. Palestine House Educational and Cultural Center (Canada)

42. Palestine Liberation Movement [Fatah]

43. Palestine Remembered (USA)

44. Palestine Right of Return Coalition (Global)

45. Palestinian Campaign for the Academic and Cultural Boycott of Israel (Palestine)

46. Palestinian Civil Society Coordinating Committee in Palestine and Abroad (Global)

47. Palestinian Liberation Front

48. Palestinian National Democratic Movement (Palestine)

49. Palestinian National Initiative

50. Palestinian People's Party

51. Palestinian Popular Struggle Front

52. Palestinian Refugee Rights Defense Committee (Balata Camp, Palestine)

53. Palestinian University Professors Union (Gaza, Palestine)

54. Palestinian Women's Grassroots Organization (Syria)

55. Palestinian Youth Democratic Union (Syria)

56. Palestinian Youth Organization (Syria)

57. Palestinian Youth Struggle Union (Syria Branch)

58. People's Assembly of the Towns and Villages Depopulated in 1948 (Palestine)

59. Platform of Associations in Solidarity with Palestine (Switzerland)

60. Popular Committees to Defend the Right of Return (Gaza, Palestine)

61. Popular Front for the Liberation of Palestine

62. Popular Front for the Liberation of Palestine - General Command

63. Refugee and Right of Return Committee (Syria)

64. Refugee Camp Popular Committees (West Bank & Gaza, Palestine)

65. Refugee Executive Office (Palestine)

66. Right of Return committee (Switzerland)

67. Ruwwad Cultural Center (Aida Camp, Palestine)

68. Salameh Association (Palestine)

69. Secular Democratic State Group (Gaza, Palestine)

70. Union of Right of Return Committees (Syria)

71. Union of Women's Activity Centers, West Bank Refugee Camps (Palestine)

72. Union of Youth Activity Centers, Refugee Camps (Palestine)

73. Vanguard for the Popular Liberation War [Sa'iqa].

74. Women's Activity Centers (Gaza, Palestine)

75. Yaffa Charitable Fund (Jordan)

76. Yaffa Cultural Center (Balata Camp, Palestine)

77. Youth Assembly (Gaza, Palestine)

78. Youth Struggle Union (Lebanon)

Table of Contents

BEST SELLERS MAX MILO EDITIONS

The Russian Art of War, Jacques Baud

Hitler's banker, Jean-François Bouchard

Confessions of a forger, Éric Piedoie Le Tiec

The Koran and the flesh, Ludovic-Mohamed Zahed

Governing by fake news, Jacques Baud

Governing by chaos, Collectif

A political history of food, Paul Ariès

Mad in U.S.A.: The ravages of the "American model",
Michel Desmurget

Mondial soccer club geopolitics, Kévin Veyssière

Putin: Game master?, Jacques Baud

Treatise on the three impostors: Moses, Jesus, Muhammad,
The Spirit of Spinoza

TV Lobotomy, Michel Desmurget